January 30, 2010

Gene —

FROM THE INSIDE-OUT
SHATTERING THE MENTAL ILLNESS MYTH. A TRUE STORY

A long time in the making but here it is.

Thanks for your words of encouragement & support over the years —

Regards —
Lawrence

From the Inside-Out: Shattering the Mental Illness Myth. A True Story by
Lauren M. Prato

Copyright © 2009 by Lauren M. Prato
BookSurge Publishing, Charleston, South Carolina.

Book Cover by: Steve Montgomery, Art Director and Designer
Cover Photo by: Terry Niefield

All rights reserved. No part of this publication may be reproduced or transmitted in any form or by any means, electronic or mechanical, including photocopy, recording, or any information storage and retrieval system, without prior written permission of the author and/or publisher.

The author does not have any intention to provide specific psychological or medical advice, but rather to provide users with information to better understand their health and/or their undiagnosed/diagnosed conditions or disorders. Please see a licensed professional with training in spiritual emergence.

Copyright © 2009 Lauren M. Prato
All rights reserved.

ISBN: 1-4392-5761-2
ISBN-13: 9781439257616

FROM THE INSIDE-OUT
SHATTERING THE MENTAL ILLNESS MYTH. A TRUE STORY

Lauren M. Prato

Dedicated to my Brother Bruce

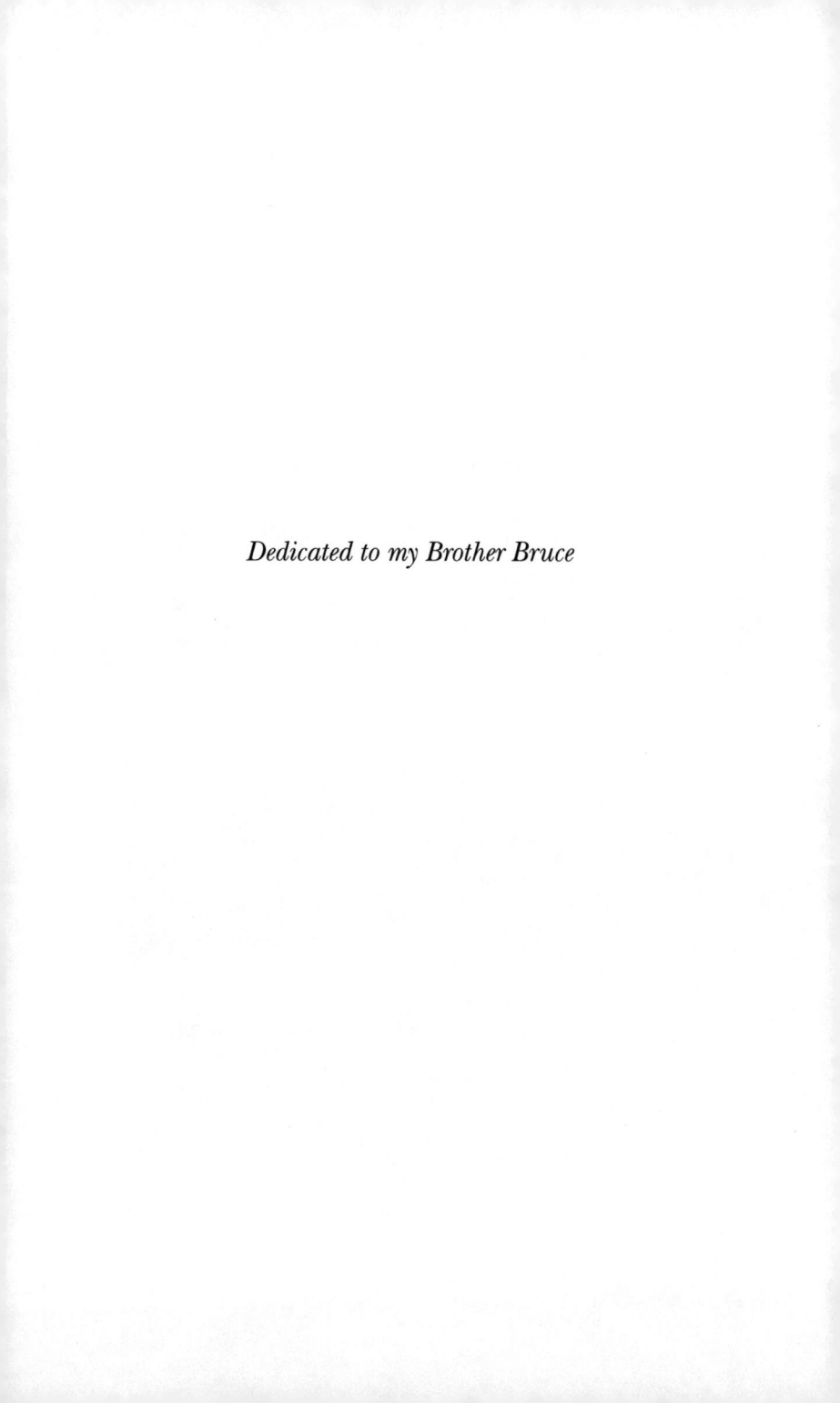

FOREWORD

Henry Grayson, Ph.D.

Lauren Prato has brought important issues to light by sharing her mental hospital experiences with us in such an open way. While we have progressed from the era of straitjackets and routine electroshock therapy, she makes us vividly aware of so many weaknesses in our care for the mentally ill. We see the lack of knowledge that would enable mental health professionals to distinguish a spiritual awakening from a psychotic episode. At least we have advanced to the degree that we do not burn people at the stake for such experiences any more.

Hospitals provide so little therapy that is helpful and healing to patients, and often the environment is not itself a healing community, as Prato points out. Being largely custodial and using medication to subdue or control undesirable behaviors, the staff is not trained to create a therapeutic community. From Lauren's experience we see the need to train, not only the custodians, but the highest levels of psychiatric and psychological professionals, to understand unusual forms of spiritual experiences, such as the rising of subtle energies as in Kundalini awakenings.

We might also raise questions about the usefulness, and sometimes harm, in operating from a strict diagnosis. When we put people in a diagnostic pigeonhole, do we box them in and therefore perpetuate their disturbance? While medication can certainly be of help to many people who are non-functioning or whose behaviors could result in harm to themselves or to others, it does not seem to bring about deeper psychological and spiritual healing, just an abatement of some symptoms.

New brain scan studies and other developments in neuropsychology show us that traumas play a very significant role in the later development of serious illnesses, both mental and physical. Yet so much of our therapeutic intervention, whether in the hospital or not, does not attend to clearing the encodings of painful information stored in the limbic system, the survival brain. From our rapidly emerging clinical experience and research, we find that there are a number of new approaches that actually work, much like deleting unwanted information from your computer. Some of these include, but are not limited to, EMDR (Eye Movement Desensitization and Reprocessing Therapy), Energy Psychology (Emotional Freedom Techniques, Tapas Acupressure Technique, Thought Field Therapy, and evolving adaptations of each), and body-based therapies. I believe there would be a significant increase in the success rate and a substantial decrease in the recidivism rate in mental hospitals, drug and alcohol rehabilitation centers, and correctional facilities if such knowledge and information were included in their treatment programs.

In spite of mounting research to the contrary, a common tendency in the mental health field is the failure to recognize the positive and strengthening effects of beliefs and spiritual and religious practices. Too often, religious beliefs and spiritual-awakening experiences are viewed only as an expression of pathology, as Lauren Prato experienced all too painfully. At the same time, we also need to be aware that there are often misuses of religious teachings that have helped create severe emotional problems as well. We must learn to distinguish between the healthy and unhealthy uses of spiritual and religious practices.

In our attempts to be scientific, we have lodged ourselves in a science that is more than three hundred years old, that of Isaac Newton, and we have not recognized the relevance of the newer sciences of the last century: quantum physics, holographic theory, field theory, brain studies, and many other related sciences such as molecular biology and botany. While these sciences have advanced in many areas of our culture, they have only slightly influenced the fields of medicine and mental health.

These studies and theories take us to an invisible but powerful realm of reality, beyond which we can study only with the five senses. We are now discovering that not only does what we think about each other have significant effects, but, especially, what we think about our patients and how we perceive them will profoundly influence the outcome of therapy. We are now finding that newer scientific discoveries have confirmed what many spiritual traditions have known for centuries—that everything and every person is interconnected in a profound yet invisible way.

I am deeply grateful to Lauren Prato for helping to make us aware of the work we mental health professionals have in front of us. May we keep our minds open and not shirk our responsibility, for we are entering a time of great reform, perhaps greater than the Copernican Revolution, where we learned that the earth was not the center of the universe.

Henry Grayson, Ph.D.
Founder and Chairman, Board of Trustees, National Institute for the Psychotherapies
Author of *Mindful Loving: 10 Practices to Deepen Your Connections* and *The New Physics of Love: The Power of Mind and Spirit in Relationships*

ACKNOWLEDGMENTS

How do you ever thank all the people who make something like this possible without missing one or forgetting some important detail? But, you have to try. Thank you first to Andy for many things and for being patient so many nights when I had to write instead of spend time with you. To my family, who I love so much, I hope you know I wrote about our family dynamics for one reason: to show the reader how those dynamics molded my personality. It was hard for me to paint any of you in a less than positive light because you are individually and collectively wonderful people, and I love you very much. I only hope I did you all justice and that you can appreciate the changes I made to your names (to protect the innocent). In no way was this book intended to hurt or portray you as less than who you are.

Thanks to John Dad for helping me reconnect with family and life. You were so right—it's tough being down here (on earth) sometimes, but here's the book I promised to write, with great thanks to you for believing in me.

To Eric Jennings, the one person who never let me down in the long process of making this story into a book with the intention of helping others. It took us three years to organize, research, and ultimately complete this arduous writing project. Thank you, thank you, thank you.

To Dr. Henry Grayson, Dr. David Lukoff, Karen Trueheart (Spiritual Emergency Network), and Gene Kieffer from the Kundalini Research Foundation, thank you for generously lending your professional expertise to this endeavor. To the many editors and artists who helped shape the book in its final form, including Edie Moser, Henry Hecht, and Sherrye Landrum, thank you for all your support and expertise.

Love always,

Lauren

TABLE OF CONTENTS

Introduction	xv
Chapter 1: Meet the Family	1
Chapter 2: Shaky Ground	7
Chapter 3: Metamorphosis	13
Chapter 4: Transformation	19
Chapter 5: Hitting the Wall	27
Chapter 6: The Big Kahuna	39
Chapter 7: The Quiet Room	57
Chapter 8: Out of the Frying Pan	77

Chapter 9: Into the Fire   85

Chapter 10: Aftermath   97

Epilogue: A Letter to My Hospital Friends   109

Appendix: 111
   DSM-IV Religious & Spiritual Problems
   by David Lukoff, Ph.D.

INTRODUCTION

The blizzard that swept through the Northeast in January 1996 had a huge impact on many people. Mention it to anyone who lived through it, and it always brings back memories. The intensity of that blizzard mirrored my own life-altering spiritual awakening. The swirling white snow seen in the twilight and the loss of visual boundaries was as profound in my inner world as it was in the changing world outside. I was deep in a new world of shifting snow drifts and shadows.

What was happening? Was it a near-death experience, a mystical transformation, a kundalini[1] awakening, or a psychological break? Whatever we decide to

---

[1] Kundalini is seen as an energy that usually resides asleep at the base of the spine. When this energy is awakened, it rises slowly up the spinal column to the top of the head. This may mark the beginning of a process of enlightenment. From *Spiritual Emergency: When Personal Transformation Becomes a Crisis*, ed. by Stanislav Grof, MD, and Christine Grof, published 1989, p. 101.

call it, I was changed for the better at a cellular, emotional, physical, and spiritual level.

The current medical model of diagnosis and treatment (with a focus on mental *illness* not mental *wellness*) categorized it as a manic episode requiring hospitalization and drug therapy. In fact, I was made a ward of the state and lost my legal rights.

There is no box to check on a mental health, medical, or insurance form for a spiritual awakening or emergency. No reimbursement code—no automatic referral for spiritual guidance. So, thousands of individuals who have had spiritual episodes like mine have also been, and continue to be, misdiagnosed, judged, ostracized, and hospitalized as mentally ill. This happens against their will and at a time when they are most vulnerable.

One of the first movies about mental illness was *The Snake Pit*, which depicted the horrifying conditions in insane asylums in the 1940s. The story was adapted from a novel by Mary Jane Ward, who knew what she was writing about because she had spent eight months in an asylum. None of the movie studios of the time wanted to touch such a story, but Daryl Zanuck took a chance. *The Snake Pit* turned out to be such an emotionally powerful film that after its release in 1948, twenty-six states changed laws regarding treatment of the mentally ill. Is that what I'm after? You bet.

In *The Snake Pit*, electroshock therapy, ice baths, and straitjackets were legitimate, even cutting-edge, treatment. I'm afraid we haven't come very far in the past sixty years. I can tell you that from firsthand experience.

There have continued to be films about mental illness, from *Three Faces of Eve* to *Girl, Interrupted*. Remember Jack Nicolson in *One Flew Over the Cuckoo's Nest*? Look beyond his sense of humor, gang of quirky patients, and successful breakout. Was that a place you would ever want to be? Me neither, but I didn't have a choice. And like Jack, I wasn't mentally ill either.

Why did the medical professionals view my spiritual emergence as requiring hospitalization and drug therapy? Because it was beyond the control or understanding of science and medicine? Because it was scary to watch?

Fear is never a good reason for extreme medical treatment. We human beings cannot go on separating our physical selves from our energy bodies and/or spiritual selves, and be whole. My hope is that this book shines a light on spiritual awakening as an essential human experience for many and alarms us all enough to consider and accept the validity of that process. I believe it is why we are born—to become more aware, to wake up, to evolve.

In an old movie, a black and white Western, a pioneer woman goes mad and can be heard singing in the ruins of a homestead all through the night. The Indians, always depicted in these old movies as savages hunting for hapless settlers, respected her madness and did not bother her. What did they know that we don't? Pretty ironic, huh?

Let me explain spiritual emergence. The terms *spiritual emergence* and *spiritual emergency* were coined by Dr. Stanislav Grof (psychiatrist) and his wife Christina Grof. They have worked for many years as therapists and researchers in the field of non-ordinary awareness and personal transformation, and they have written many books about spiritual emergence. I refer you to two of their books, *Spiritual Emergency: When Personal*

Transformation Becomes a Crisis and *The Stormy Search for the Self: A Guide to Personal Growth through Transformational Crisis.* The growing number of transpersonal psychiatrists and psychologists in our country attests to their success in educating others about this natural process.

We humans have experiences that can be labeled spiritual, religious, or simply out of the ordinary. These could be as simple as walking in nature and seeing light glowing in every living thing or as complex as the visions and levitations of a saint. In each experience, an individual has personally come in contact with holy ground, and such experiences can change us and the way we look at our own lives.

But they are difficult to explain to others—especially people who have not had similar experiences. If the experience brings up more psychological material than we can deal with on our own, the spiritual emergence becomes an *emergency.* That emergency can manifest in a number of ways. Should a person undergoing such an experience have no support system, it may be wise to consult a physician, psychologist, or even a psychiatrist—particularly one that is *familiar with spiritual emergency issues.*

As we'll see, most mental health practitioners are completely unschooled in this area and are trained, indeed, to consider it a mental illness, or worse, a permanent state of being, needing life-long treatment. Such myths and misperceptions need to be addressed and corrected. That is the point of what follows.

Little emphasis has been placed on the positives of these life-altering events. In fact, there is a great likelihood they can be integrated and celebrated as another milestone on one's life journey.

For My Family

I love my family. They are, individually and collectively, wonderful people. I write about our family dynamics for one reason: development of my character to show the reader how those dynamics molded my personality. The foundation of many of my emotional strengths and weaknesses was forged on those dynamics and interactions. My sole intention is to aid readers to understand the development of my personality.

Lauren Prato, 2009

Chapter 1:
MEET THE FAMILY

I have been living outside the box for most of my adult life. You might ask, "What does that mean?" Briefly, it means that most of the time, traditional modes of healing, such as medicine, mainstream doctors, and psychotherapy, just didn't work for me. I inevitably sought natural modes of therapy and healing for everything from a bruise to a fracture—in short, almost anything related to my wellness.

What was so wrong with that? Why did I need all this help on my personal journey anyway? That's a loaded question—and by the way, we all need help on the journey. My journey begins with my family.

My arrival into the world resulted in a state of crisis for me, my mother, and the hospital (I guess an Aries triple-fire sign couldn't arrive in any less dramatic way). My mother almost died giving birth to me. I was whisked away and not brought to her for many hours.

(Occasionally, I teasingly remind her that she abandoned me at a very early age.)

I was the fifth of six children, all boys but me: Michael, then Kenneth, who died of pneumonia at ten days old, followed by Brad, Larry, me (born on my parents' seventh anniversary), and Craig. We were a typical American family of the 1950s and 1960s.

My mother, Conchetta, is Italian/Hungarian. Her mother was born in Hungary and died in the United States when I was four. Her father was first generation from Naples; he was born in New York City and died from Hodgkin's Disease before I was born. Conchetta always told me what a perfect childhood she had. She was bright and cheerful with loving, happily married parents, and she excelled in everything she did— Valedictorian of her high school class, super-athlete, most popular, beautiful, artistically inclined, and at sixteen, she was able to sew the most fashionable clothing of her day, using sophisticated Vogue patterns. She was a very hard act to follow.

Dad was a good provider and worked two jobs as a New York City firefighter and a shoe salesman. He demanded quiet at home and lacked patience, particularly after two nights on duty at the firehouse. With five kids, how he expected peace and quiet was beyond us. After dinner, he always made a quick exit to the living room and buried himself in the newspaper, not to be heard from for hours. When that paper went up, we kept out.

Raised in Yonkers by Sicilian Catholic parents, my dad was quirky, and his troubled family history (hidden from us until we were adults) influenced our family dynamics. More on that later.

I grew up with many cousins. There were usually fifteen of us plus adults at family outings, yet one of my earliest memories is feeling like I didn't fit in with my female cousins. I was much more comfortable with the boys, and I felt like an outcast around other girls. (With four brothers, that seems natural now, but it was a big deal for me then.)

Although you wouldn't know it now, I was extremely shy, insecure, and nervous in any social setting. I clung to my mother and was deathly afraid of almost everything, most notably grown men.

Cat-licks

In our very Catholic family, we said prayers at bedtime with my mother kneeling next to us. We prayed to a stern God, who lived up in heaven. I was afraid of doing something wrong and being punished. It wasn't possible to connect to this God on a personal level. He seemed judgmental, powerful, and very far away.

My Sixth Sense

I was born with spiritual aptitudes, such as clairvoyance, that, to me, had nothing to do with the God I just described. I didn't learn how to do these things from my mother or the church; they were just a natural part of me. For example, I could tell her who was calling as the phone rang, and I was almost always right. My mother thought my abilities came from my Hungarian grandmother, who had similar gifts. We girls—me, my mother, and my grandmother's spirit—spent every Sunday in the kitchen cooking. (In an Italian-American family, the boys got Sundays off while the girls cooked all day. This was not optional.)

One of our favorite pastimes was "what's in this dish?" This meant I'd have to guess which spices she was adding. I was right from a very early age, much to my mother's puzzlement. I credit my grandmother for this too.

Another gift—if you want to call it that—is my stomach's ability to act as a warning system. One day, as the town's fire horn blew at an unscheduled time, I felt nauseated with fear and panic. I knew something had happened to someone close to me. We soon learned that my brother had been in a serious car accident, broken his neck, and was in the hospital. The whistle had blown the alert for Larry's accident. (Luckily, he made a complete recovery.)

I also believed that I had been reincarnated. In fact, I believed I had been a horse. My mother said I shared that belief with my grandmother too (not the horse part, the reincarnation part).

I don't know how other children think about these things, but I was always certain I had a purpose for being born. It wasn't just going to school, being a Brownie, and fitting in with expectations of what girls should be. I knew I had a mission here on earth, even though I didn't yet know what it would be. (I have since learned and I believe that all of us have a purpose for coming to earth.)

Ugly Duckling

My brothers were typical boys. They played endless pranks and jokes on me. I was hopelessly outnumbered and teased incessantly. They mocked my most sensitive issues, and there were quite a few.

I was tall for my age and heavy, a.k.a., "fat." I had a deeper voice than most girls, a.k.a., a "man voice." I also had thick, unmanageable hair, common for females sharing a Mediterranean background, a.k.a., "hairy." I was left-handed; my brothers were all right-handed. I even had a special seat at the dinner table, so as not to bump elbows with anyone.

At school things weren't much better. I was an average student and struggled with reading, comprehension and writing, a.k.a., "dumb." Being left-handed was a clear handicap according to the nuns, a.k.a., "hand of the Devil." As the tallest girl, I was forever ordered to the back of the line. The cute shorter girls, adored by the nuns, were way in front of me. It was bad enough to be in the back of the line, but my height also put me at the rear of the class. Talk about feeling ostracized.

There was no escape. Even the neighborhood kids seized every opportunity to remind me that I didn't fit in. The petite girls teased me like my brothers did. They called me names like "Scarlet O'Hairy," and "Monkey Trunky Donkey." I admit they were colorful, but this was so hurtful it affected me for years. On the surface, however, I was stoic, to show them they hadn't gotten to me.

So, it's no wonder my earliest memories are laced with feelings of sadness and lethargy. Compared to my four outrageously energetic brothers, I was the inert center of a whirlwind of activity. I was lonesome and different. There was only one conclusion for me to make: something was wrong.

My mother made some short-lived attempts to get me to socialize with other girls: Brownies lasted a month and the Girl Scouts for one brief, torturous day. I felt like a fish out of water. I begged my mother not to take me back.

At eight years of age, I began to manifest emotional problems. I was panicked at the thought of being alone. Leaving my mother's side for any reason created enormous stress as though I were being cast to the wolves. I was insecure and filled with self-loathing.

Looking back, these tumultuous feelings resulted in what I would now describe as the beginnings of anxiety and depression.

Chapter 2:
SHAKY GROUND

Hormone Hell

Puberty began at ten, earlier than any of the other girls at school. My already overgrown, overweight body changed rapidly. I grew taller, my skin broke out, and my breasts grew noticeably— sometimes, it seemed, by the minute. My growing pains were literal; at times it felt like I was being stabbed with sharp, painful blows to my breast.

As if that weren't enough, my brothers seized puberty as another opportunity for colorful name-calling, adding "shark nose" and "Big Bertha" to the repertoire. I felt gross.

Mixed messages about food from my mother didn't help. On the one hand, she was a phenomenal cook, producing feasts that emphasized food as love. On the other, having me counting calories in the second grade was a strong indicator that fat was ugly. Conchetta would say things like, "Take the laundry downstairs; you'll burn two calories," or "Take out the trash; you'll burn four calories." The more importance she placed on burning calories, the more resentful and consumed with food I became.

The more womanly my body became, the more distant my father was. Before puberty, he had called me Chiquita ("little girl" in Spanish), but then he stopped and became uncomfortable around me. He treated me as an extension of my mother. Our relationship depended on how he was getting along with her. If they were on good terms, great. If they weren't, he ignored me. He did not do this to my brothers. It seemed as though the house was divided into two camps.

As usual, my brothers didn't help matters. To them, girlish beauty did not include a twelve-year-old with size 8½ shoes and a deep voice. I started to accept their ridicule as truth. I rejected femininity and sank deeper into envying the short, thin, miniskirted girls at school.

Cutting the Apron Strings

When I was in fourth grade, my mother had a falling out with the Roman Catholic Church over birth control, took us out of Catholic school, and put us in public school. We stopped going to church. My uniform days were over, and my eyes were opened to the world of fashion: makeup, hairdos, pierced ears, trendy clothes. I was a kid turned loose in a candy store with so many choices. My new look caused more than raised eyebrows with both parents. My father forbade me to wear miniskirts or pierce my ears. We fought for months. I wanted to fit in, so I solved one problem by rolling up my skirt when I got to school—until Conchetta caught me. It became such a huge issue that I eventually only wore pants.

Facing up to my fathers strictness, I felt anger and defiance well up in me for the first time in my life. I was not going to give in, no matter what. I had never acted this way before, never voiced my desires before. The good little girl was gone.

My mother encouraged me to dress more feminine. She wanted me to wear dresses and lace; I wanted to wear chukkas and jeans. My bedroom had pink walls, white eyelet, and a canopy bed, and I hated it. She wanted a ladylike daughter who knew how to sew and cook; I was too tough, outspoken, and witty.

Eventually, my rebelliousness and outspokenness led to showdowns with Conchetta. Our arguments ended with her grabbing a wooden spoon or a brush. As I grew, her choice of props grew too. Rolling pins from the kitchen drawer propelled me out the back door, running for dear life. Boy, could she run! She would chase me around the property. Most of the time, I outran her. Once caught, a catfight would begin, which might include her pulling my hair. At that point, I'd drop like a rock onto my back and start kicking my legs in rapid succession, like a propeller. She was defenseless—and I got another lesson in personal power.

I refused to let her (or anyone) see me cry or know she had caused me pain. I did everything I could to hold back tears when we fought. I was a classic stoic—a time-honored technique for dealing with one's family, but it was expensive emotionally.

Best Friends

Then I met Marybeth, two years older, 5'10", and blond. Although we were both tall, our differences ran deep. I came from a meticulously kept home with overly protective parents; she came from an unkempt home with older parents, and alcoholism ran rampant in the family.

Marybeth was confident and inspiring—instrumental in my development into an independent individual. She was a sounding board and gave me courage to defy my parents. She was my first best friend. We became inseparable.

Then, just when I thought my brothers had exhausted all the names they could call me, they called me a lesbo (a lesbian). This didn't faze Marybeth. She was beyond us all in confidence. And she had a razor-sharp tongue that even the guys feared. With Marybeth in the same school, I could eat lunch with her every day, and my social anxiety eased significantly.

Shaky Ground

Then, to my horror, my middle school was divided from the high school. Marybeth, who was in high school, was gone. I was petrified. My deepest fear was back—I was alone. The loss of Marybeth triggered anxiety, insomnia, and panic attacks. My over-attachment to my mother returned. I developed a chronically upset stomach and lost weight.

Exhausted from lack of sleep, I was cranky, even nasty at school. The insomnia got worse, and it became more difficult to do schoolwork. By bedtime, my stomach would be twisted into knots. The same chain of events recurred night after night. First, it was time for bed. I would feel panicky, as though I were suffocating. My mind would race. I would be consumed by thoughts of the misery at school and the loss of Marybeth. As the night went on, I would begin to feel I was the only one awake in the house, the neighborhood, the state, the country, and even the world. It was just me and me alone. I had no idea how irrational I was.

I would often wake my mother, who was patient and empathetic. She would lie beside me and rock me to sleep, massaging my head, coaching me to think of happy thoughts and good times. Sometimes she would sing and hum. She tried everything.

My father, on the other hand, grew angry about my mother leaving his bedside. Her time with me seemed to make him unreasonably jealous. Tension between my mother and father grew.

One morning before school, I had a meltdown. Exhausted and emotionally raw, I began to sob. Soon, my mother broke down too. For the first time, I could see the toll this was taking on her. She, too, looked exhausted. She was desperate; she had done everything she knew, and it pained her to see me so unhappy. "Perhaps we should seek professional help," she said.

Chapter 3:
METAMORPHOSIS

To me, having to see a "shrink" meant something was seriously wrong. My oldest brother had seen a psychologist when he was younger, and believe me, I did not want to be like him. This was like being slapped in the face. I decided to deal with my fears on my own.

Transformation #1

I had many talks with myself. I didn't want to be miserable anymore; I didn't want to be nasty. I wanted to be popular, and I wanted to be happy, thin, and smart, like the popular girls at school.

I learned to overcome insomnia by altering my thoughts. I imagined being funny and well-liked at school. Eventually, I developed a vision of myself; one of a beautiful, slender, elegantly dressed woman wearing a black gown with diamond earrings descending a circular stairway. An adoring crowd watches from below, admiring and applauding her success and fame. In my vision, I am completely and utterly beautiful-from the inside out.

By the next school year, I had lost the excess weight and decided never to be overweight again. How? I would simply deprive myself of food until it stopped controlling my life. I lost twenty-three pounds. Granted, it was not the healthiest way to go, but I did create a permanent, positive shift in my relationship with food. Food became less of an obsession, and although I occasionally binged, I never relied on food to make me feel loved again.

At school, I began playing volleyball and running track. This helped keep my body in shape. I stayed after school to study and improve my grades, always did the extra-credit assignments, and achieved and maintained honors. I fit in with most everyone; my friends were an eclectic group, including jocks, heads, bad girls, dweebs, nerds, and the super smart. I was well on my way to achieving my vision.

First Love

I often questioned why I couldn't get a date during high school. I didn't know until years later that my brothers had intimidated most of the guys at school who might have had any romantic interest in me. So when my friend Fran introduced me to a boy named Matthew from another school, I was thrilled.

Matthew and I had an instant attraction for each other. For me, it was love at first sight. There was one problem—okay, maybe many problems. Matthew was a year older, went to our rival high school, drank alcohol, was a partier, smoked pot, and had an explosive temper. In short, he was from the wrong side of the tracks. My family was terribly upset. They were determined to break us up.

My mother relentlessly proclaimed that virginity was the highest virtue for any girl. She would have provided me with a chastity belt stamped with the word "virgin" if she could have. She reminded me that she knew only too well what seventeen-year-old boys had in mind, and it wasn't love.

Naturally, the more Conchetta harped on me about sex, the more curious I became. I began to explore with Matthew, although he never scored the home run he was after. I stayed with him through my senior year, and with Matthew in tow, I graduated in June 1977.

College

That fall, I entered Fordham University as a pre-med student. In spite of a rigorous pre-med curriculum, I played on the varsity volleyball team, kept my relationship with Matthew, and worked on weekends.

Not being a gifted student, my grades began to suffer and things began to unravel quickly. The pre-med schedule was extremely demanding, and I quickly lost interest. To complicate matters, Matthew did not change for the better (what a surprise!). The summer after my freshman year, I broke up with him. I began my sophomore year still devastated from the breakup with Matthew. Although I knew it was the right thing to do, it was one of the most difficult decisions of my life.

As for my parents, the friction I had first seen as a child continued escalating. Finally, my mother served my father with divorce papers. Almost immediately, however, they reconciled.

After a frustrating, uninspiring sophomore year, I switched to the fastest track to graduation-sociology. During summer break, I backpacked through Europe with two college friends. I was nineteen years old, so getting my parents to agree to the trip wasn't easy. But I convinced them.

My newfound independence during the trip was life-altering and exhilarating. I had a surge of confidence, and when I returned, I moved into an off-campus apartment. It was a small place with three other roommates, but the independence and sense of adventure overcame even the roaches and substandard conditions.

Conchetta Leaves Gaetano: Take Two

During the early part of my junior year, my mother served a second set of divorce papers to my father. I was supportive of her decision.

By February, they had again reconciled, to my distress. My mother tried to make me understand. She explained that my father had become more and more desperate and had threatened suicide. I didn't understand the significance of the threat until she told me the real story of how my father became an orphan. Like most family secrets, what she revealed pulled the rug out from under me.

I had been told that my father's parents died in a car accident and that he was separated from his siblings and passed from relative to relative. In reality, my father's father, who was thirteen years older than his wife, accused her of infidelity and shot her. Then he used the gun on himself. My eleven-year-old father found both parents dead. I cannot imagine the devastating effect this must have had on him as a young boy, and I could see that my father's threat could not be ignored. I was also sure this reconciliation would not change anything.

Still, the truth had shaken me to the core. I retreated to my room that night and sobbed. My brother Craig came to check on me, and I cried myself to sleep in his arms. A bond was sealed that night. Craig became my protector, guide, and caretaker.

The remainder of the school year was difficult. I felt disconnected and apathetic, unhappy with the curriculum and uninspired by most of my professors. I struggled with bouts of depression, anger, and feeling lost.

Love and Graduation

In the beginning of my senior year, I met and fell in love with an incredible man, Sean. He was my first healthy, significant love relationship.

By the end of the year, Sean asked me to marry him, but he lived in Ireland and I lived here. Being just twenty-one, I felt unable to leave the United States to live with him abroad. Neither could he see himself leaving his home country.

Soon after we parted, I graduated. The year was 1981.

The Divorce

After a bitter separation, Conchetta finally divorced my father. She filled her new life with activity, but harbored a lot of resentment and anger. After the divorce, family life disintegrated, which I hadn't anticipated. For each of us, it was a time to adjust to painful emotions.

Chapter 4:
TRANSFORMATION

Manhattan, The Real World

After Fordham, I was given an incredible opportunity to move to New York City's Upper West Side, with my college roommate. Like all twenty-somethings living in Manhattan at the time, I wanted to make a lot of money, and I thought medical sales would be the most lucrative.

I worked a few short-term jobs and even worked in marketing in a prominent sports marketing firm before I eventually landed my first sales job for a distributor in health and beauty aids/pharmaceuticals.

Finally, at twenty-seven years old, I was hired for my first "real" job, selling pharmaceuticals with a major corporation. I had hit the big league, with a great salary, company car, and expense account.

Throughout my twenties, I held on to the vision I had created as a young girl—to be my personal best. Success in my vision meant having a successful career with a fit body, being smart and confident, having a great partner, and making a difference. I was determined to have it all.

I paid little attention to my psychological or spiritual self up to this point. At twenty-seven, having chalked up a few more failed relationships, depression and discontentment loomed. Living the high life in Manhattan with a good job and a promising future didn't prevent them. There was a never-ending feeling that something was wrong in my life. Something was missing. I knew I had to do something more. To be that woman in my vision, I had to search further. There was no other option.

NYC Burnout

After nine years in Manhattan, I felt worn down and depleted. The filth of the city got to me. Then I fractured my back in a serious bike accident in Central Park. The recuperation period gave me time to think. I needed a change—I desperately desired quiet, nature, and a cleaner environment. So, I bought my first home. It was close to the city and my family but gave me enough distance to maintain my hard-earned independence.

I had not seen or spoken to my father in eight years. My relationship with my brothers was friendly but not very deep. Craig, my closest friend in the family, joined the Air Force, got married, and moved away. I felt yet another enormous sense of loss.

Soon after, I ended a year-long relationship. I plunged into loneliness and despair. I knew that there had to be a way to move beyond this phase.

Transformation #2

At work, I noticed that a colleague was making positive, significant changes in her life. She told me about a program called The Forum, offered by a company called Landmark Education Corporation. She said The Forum had stimulated her to make these changes, and encouraged me to join her. As her guest, I attended an introductory workshop. The evening was strange, but I signed up anyway.

The Forum, an intensive two-weekend workshop, provided the next level of positive change in my life, equal in every way to my adolescent transformation. After the workshop, I was in a state of elation and heightened awareness. Colors seemed more intense; life seemed passionate and exciting. I felt I was in control of my life and my environment. There was no hint of depression for weeks. I was living life without limits. What a rush!

The Forum focused on having a choice in EVERY aspect of our lives, as simple (in theory) as choosing between chocolate or vanilla. The Forum also strongly encouraged resolving family relationships.

As a result, I contacted my father for the first time in ten years, and visited him at the shoe store he now owned. It was a new beginning for our relationship.

The Forum produces, for some individuals, rapid change. Unfortunately, any kind of rapid change can scare others, especially family members. When my mother and cousin attended closing ceremonies, I realize, in retrospect, this had to be overwhelming for them. All of us graduates were bursting with over-the-top excitement. It must have looked very strange to them, scary in fact.

Although I was devastated by my mother's reaction, teachers at The Forum assured me that having a relationship with your family—no matter what—is a key component to healing your past and moving beyond your issues. Ultimately, I would have to be the one to reconcile any differences between my mother and myself.

The Forum catapulted me into doing things I wouldn't have done otherwise, yet after a few weeks, the elation subsided, the newness was gone, and I felt like my old self again. It was a bit of a disappointment coming back to reality. I thought my depression had been cured. Being a novice at this kind of transformation, I expected a permanent personality shift and hoped that the end of my depression was part of that shift, but it returned and snapped me back into reality. Quite a letdown![2]

It didn't help to tell Conchetta about reconnecting with my father. She was furious and convinced that The Forum had brainwashed me. Little did she know that Craig had made peace with him too. In fact, Craig and I thought perhaps it would be less painful for everyone if my parents forgave each other and remarried.

When Conchetta found out that Craig had also seen dad, she was enraged. She set out to convince me

---

[2] From a chapter by Roberto Assagioli in the Grof's book *Spiritual Emergency*, p. 27–48: Such a state of exalted joy may last for varying periods, but it is bound to cease. The inflow of light and love is rhythmical, as is everything in the universe. After a while it diminishes or ceases, and the flood is followed by the ebb. The personality was infused and transformed, but this transformation is seldom either permanent or complete. More often a large portion of the personality elements involved revert to their earlier state.

that I needed professional help. There was no appeasing her until I agreed to see someone, so for the first time in my life, I went to the yellow pages and called a therapist.

She was a traditional therapist, soft-spoken, with a nurturing tone. Over the next year, she helped me see my life differently. She encouraged me to question my relationship with my mother in ways I had never considered. Ironically, we concluded that my mother was much more of an issue in my life than The Forum, cult or not. She helped me to see my mother as a human being for the first time, complete with her own baggage. I began to understand her need to control me, my life, and everything around her. I saw how suffocating our relationship was for both of us. Perhaps my mother, too, could benefit from therapy.

The therapist recommended some self-help books, especially about mother-daughter relationships, and I plunged into books, articles, and discussions with friends.

I also attended several Forum follow-up seminars and advanced courses. That was where I met Lynette. We connected immediately, joking about our life plans and how we would like to be married by a particular date. A group photo was taken, and I said it looked like a wedding photo. She could have been my sister-in-law, except all my brothers were married. (One year later, unbeknownst to me, she met my brother Craig, who had separated from his wife. A few years later, they married. How's that for a cosmic coincidence!)

Several of my classmates and I made a commitment to go skydiving. We drove to upstate New York and tandem-jumped 13,500 feet. I was petrified. Mike, my instructor, offered two choices: "Either pass out or make this the most exciting adventure of your life."

Standing at the door, strapped to the jumpmaster and feeling sheer terror, I suddenly saw my "light body" walk ahead of me and jump out of the plane. All fear left me. I walked to the door, said, "Oh my God, she did it," and jumped.

The free fall was beyond my wildest imagination. In those forty-five explosive seconds, I experienced exuberance, heart palpitations, the rush of the wind, and exhilaration from the speed at which I was falling. I thought pulling the cord was going to be the end of the excitement, but there was one more thrill in store. We landed standing up in the middle of the target, a perfect landing. It *was* the most thrilling adventure of my life.

Still, I didn't think much about the out-of-body experience. My life continued to change, as Landmark predicted it would. Friends supported my personal growth with encouragement and more books[3]. I also began journaling and meditating.

Although I loved the pharmaceutical company I worked for and the people I worked with, I grew to resent the culture of the industry. The drug companies often wined, dined, and encouraged doctors to use pharmaceuticals as the solution for medical problems that should have been initially addressed through diet, nutrition, and exercise, three all-important lifestyle changes for good health.

---

[3] I read *The Celestine Prophecy*, *The Artist's Way*, Marianne Williamson's *Return to Love*, the *Course in Miracles*, and several other books that opened my heart and my worldview.

As I grew more committed to the path of natural, drug-free, alternative health, I found myself in a constant struggle about staying in the pharmaceutical industry. I began to explore other careers more in line with my values, which included nutrition and exercise, with overall wellness as the primary focus.

Lynette referred me for a position as a medical device rep and technical support in a major orthopedic company. This was a great opportunity to transition out of pharmaceutical sales and launched me into one of the most challenging jobs of my life. There were few women in this field, and proving myself interested me, especially when I was told by men in the business, "You'll never make it." This only inspired me more. Type A personality? You bet.

I faced tremendous challenges. I was, once again, in a male-dominated world, and I felt the need to be aggressive and stick up for myself. I talked tough and acted tough, but most of the managers denigrated my abilities. In fact, they harassed me. I was accused of sleeping with my clients, wearing provocative clothing to get business, and not learning the more than ten thousand products quickly enough.

It proved to be much more than I bargained for. Within weeks I was consumed by fear and feelings of inadequacy. I had bouts of crying and meltdowns. I wanted to quit.

Serendipity

During this time, my oldest brother Michael was arrested for drunk driving and admitted to a rehabilitation center not far from my mother's home. The family was asked to attend therapy as part of his recovery process. The counselor, Lois, was quick to pick up on our family dynamics. During the family session, Lois and I clicked, and given my deplorable work situation, I made an appointment to see her privately.

Lois helped me realize that I had recreated a pattern at work similar to the one I grew up with—the only girl in a man's world, the target of criticism and rejection. With her help, I was able to choose to explore and express my feminine side. I used to joke that I didn't realize I was a woman until I was in my thirties, but it was true.

After the internal work with Lois, I felt able to take on the challenges of the job with more confidence and security. Good fortune also played a role—or was it part of the personal growth? The intolerable managers were let go, and my best buddy became my boss.

Chapter 5:
HITTING THE WALL

Digging a Little Too Deep?

After these successful sessions with Lois, I felt ready to probe a little deeper into my issues. I was referred to a well-known rather unconventional therapist, Sandy. His eclectic sessions focused on transferring emotions from feelings into physical actions. It was very intense and helped me verbalize my continuing depression and anger, which I called the "black hole."

While it had an overall positive effect, work with Sandy also stimulated deeply submerged issues that led to deeper bouts of depression. After about six months, I decided Sandy's process was too painful to continue.

I decided to stop working with a therapist for a while and explore my inner conflicts in a less formalized way. But the more I persevered, the deeper into the hole I went.

As part of my continued spiritual exploration, I began attending services at an Episcopal church near my home, and I grew to love the atmosphere there. It had been a long time since I was part of an organized church community. The magnificent organ music and voices of the choir touched me deeply. Still, my emotions were raw, and I continued to feel vulnerable, hopeless and depressed.

Gradually, my interest in spirituality led me to metaphysics and "alternative" health practices. The Forum had opened me up to considering new ideas. I was avidly reading, taking classes and participating in workshops. My beliefs shifted.

My spiritual philosophy became an eclectic mix of Eastern and Western principles, including yoga/meditation, Buddhism and even Native American traditions. My search deepened into a personal, introspective journey.

One weekend, my friend Marie and I took a workshop called Exceptional Cancer Patients[4]. The workshop consisted of dealing with the realities of people's mortality, fear, and pain. It also focused on visualization processes and self-analysis through drawing and prayer. The workshop proved to be profound and life-altering in its depth and exploration of the topic. After the workshop, Marie invited me to her house to meet her father. He and I had an immediate connection. We even felt that her father and I had met in a former life.

Months later, I signed up for a six-week visualization seminar, to learn how to use visualizations to create the life I wanted. During that time, I was reading

---

[4] Given by Dr. Bernie Siegel at the Omega Institute in Rhinebeck, New York.

voraciously[5]. I also took an Anthony Robbins "Breaking Through" course. For inner cleansing, I did hydro-colon therapy (colonics) and continued to tweak my nutritional supplements and diet. I also studied Kung Fu and remained current with the latest body sculpting and weight-training techniques.

I continued to pray for a miraculous transformation. I re-evaluated many aspects of my life: undesirable habits had to go, or I had to find out why I was sustaining them. I did a lot of work releasing the negativity and self-loathing that had continued to build since childhood. I dug into the sources of my depression. I agonized over wanting to be compassionate. I wanted to connect and contribute to the lives of other people. In spite of all these efforts, at age thirty-six, I was still battling chronic depression.

My mother insisted that my non-mainstream therapies had clouded my judgment. She asserted that my moodiness and depressive disposition were genetic, that I inherited them from my *father's* side of the family. She pointed to the tragic deaths of my grandparents, the numerous hospitalizations of Aunt Maria—including electric shock treatments—and my permanently shell-shocked Vietnam-vet cousin. Add the frequent, reclusive moods of my father, and you get a recipe for hereditary depression.

---

[5] I read Carlos Castenada's *The Secret Teachings of Don Juan*; Harville Hendricks's *Getting the Love You Want*; Brian Weiss's *Many Lives, Many Masters*; and *Embraced by the Light* by Betty J. Eadie and Curtis Taylor. I read books by Wayne Dyer, Deepak Chopra, and Barbara DeAngelis. I read Dan Millman's *Way of the Peaceful Warrior* and met him when he spoke at St. Bart's in Manhattan. I also read several of Marianne Williamson's books and attended her lectures.

When pressed, Conchetta acknowledged a bit of alcoholism and drug addiction in her family. She suggested that I, like my brother, Michael, might have a chemical imbalance and could be helped with medication. She didn't believe my depression could be overcome by alternative medicine or New Age hocus pocus.[6] In her mind, I would not improve unless I was medicated.

To appease her and to continue my quest for a cure, I gave in. Perhaps my mother was right after all. Deep down, I knew taking prescription drugs to control depression was not for me, but I had exhausted all my options.

Diagnosis: Bipolar, Depressed, and Devastated

My cousin Jenn, my closest relative and friend at the time, recommended her psychotherapist. During our one and only session, the doctor said he couldn't believe I had not been medicated. I was immediately sent across the hall to the austere yet pretentious office of a psychiatrist, Dr. Wachs. Within fifteen minutes I was diagnosed as manic-depressive and given a prescription for Lithium.

My heart sank. Against my intuition and steadfast beliefs, I decided to give drug therapy six months. I rationalized that at the end of six months, I could do as I pleased.

The sessions with Dr. Wachs were bleak. He would lean his head back in his red leather chair, close his eyes,

---

[6] She reminded me that Michael had been diagnosed with bipolar disorder and had been taking Thorazine, Stelazine, and Lithium for years. It didn't seem to matter that he also suffered liver damage and developed diabetes.

and chew incessantly on the end of a straw as if I were boring the living life out of him. I felt utter despair and frustration. I confronted him, asserting he wasn't listening. To appease me, Dr. Wachs responded by stating that in his own therapy, it had taken four sessions a week for somewhere between five and seven years before he got results. A quick calculation would mean approximately eighteen years of sessions and Lithium for me to see a lasting result. Stick a pencil in my eye!

Even though I concluded that Dr. Wachs was less than skilled and appeared to be medicated himself, I filled the prescription. After a few weeks, I didn't feel any improvement. In fact, I only recall unpleasant side effects, which began early and continued throughout my course of treatment. A metallic smell pervaded my body, I gained weight, and I lost my ability to feel or express emotions, good or bad. I felt emotionally numb, apathetic, and detached, as if someone had placed a lid on my emotions. Rather than leveling out my feelings or helping me, I began to feel capped: not sad, not happy, not anything. I was among the walking dead.

I did everything I could to combat the side effects. I worked out feverishly in the gym, but my weight wouldn't budge, and the toxic smell coming from my body, particularly when I perspired, wouldn't go away. It took everything I had to get myself to work out under these conditions.

In May of 1995, I went on a bicycle vacation through Tuscany with a friend from work. Given how much I loved Italy, I would have normally felt excited and exuberant, yet I was entirely removed and nearly catatonic. I couldn't feel anything. I remained emotionally detached and frustrated. This was worse than being depressed. When I returned home, I was certain I could not remain on Lithium.

Trying my best to keep my promise to use drug therapy for six months, I continued one final month with Dr. Wachs. I was miserable, both from him and the drugs. If I thought my vacation was the pits, sessions with Wachs put me at rock bottom. More and more, my instinct was to dump Wachs and Lithium and return to my original search for spiritually-based treatments.

Back on Track: Alternative Therapy

One afternoon, while at my chiropractor's office, I saw an advertisement in a holistic guidebook for alternative therapists. Katy, a spiritual healer, was trained and certified by the Barbara Brennan School, famous for alternative approaches to emotional and spiritual healing. Her ad mentioned depression, family issues, and alcoholism. It seemed a good fit, and her office was near my home.

My heart warmed when I called her. Katy's voice was soft, resonant, and calm. I felt the presence of God's love immediately. Katy brought a sense of safety and comfort to the conversation, something that the psychiatrist never provided. She didn't rush, and she gave me her undivided attention. She listened. I felt she would be a wonderful counselor, but I didn't blindly trust Katy in the beginning (or anyone who worked on me). By that I mean I was just as wary of spiritual therapists as I was of those with a psychiatric background. By this point, I was leery of all claims of healing and cures. Proof would come with time.

I kept my promise and finished out my time with Dr. Wachs. I told him Lithium was deepening my depression, and he decreased the dosage, trying to ease the problem.

In what became my last visit, he closed his eyes, chewed on his straw, and tuned out. My blood boiled. I told him one last time that I felt the drug was making me more depressed. And he said, "You know, I really don't think you're bipolar. I think you're depressed." Duh!!! His solution was Prozac. He recommended I continue the Lithium and add Prozac! Stick another pencil in my eye!

This made no sense whatsoever. What could he be thinking? I was devastated. Prozac was at the bottom of my list of solutions. The bad press and Prozac-related suicides sprang to mind. It took days for me to fill the prescription.

The first day on Prozac, I felt wired and out of control. I was short-tempered, and I snapped at people, which was totally out of character.

To hell with Prozac and Dr. Wachs. I stopped taking Prozac and ended my relationship with him and Lithium. I vowed to heal without drugs and focused my energy on healing work with Katy.

Coming Home: A Spiritual Approach

Sessions with Katy had three parts: counseling, energy work, and debriefing. During the counseling portion, Katy encouraged me to explore my psychological issues and pain. She was a wonderful listener. I was truly being heard.

Energy work was done on the massage table. First, she would smudge the room.[7] Then she began the

---

[7] Smudging is done with dried sage, considered a sacred herb in Native American traditions. Once lit, the smoke is diffused,

hands-on treatment. With my eyes closed, she held her hands above my body, working with my chakras[8]. I would see vivid colors: indigo blue, purple, green, or sometimes, red. Emotions would arise. I might cry, feel grief sadness, or incredible peace, serenity, and love. I would experience pressure, heat, tingling, or vibrations as her hands touched various parts of my body.

At the debriefing, I would tell her what I experienced on the table. She gave clarity to my feelings and sensations, encouraging me to trust myself. I felt validated. I always left her sessions feeling peaceful. She was God-sent.

The Shadow Self

Katy taught me about Carl Jung's concept of the Shadow Self[9]. She said our shadow selves are an important part

---

cleansing negativity from the room. The aroma of sage is pleasing to the Great Spirit and abhorred by evil spirits.

[8] Briefly, chakras are energy centers located along the spine. According www.barbarabrennan.com, **"This is a hands-on healing system that works with an individual's energy consciousness system to promote physical, emotional, mental, and spiritual health."**

[9] The Shadow is a term introduced by Carl G. Jung. It contains the parts of us that are unconscious, repressed, undeveloped, and denied. There are both light and dark aspects of our being, so there is positive undeveloped potential in the Shadow as well as negative. We confront the Shadow to become self-aware. We cannot learn about ourselves if we do not look at our Shadow. Summarized from *The Shadow Dance: Understanding Repetitive Patterns in Relationships* by Rebeca E. Eigen, *Indigo Sun* magazine, August 1999, online at www.indigosun.com.

of each of us and may include sub-selves. One might be called the depressed self; another might be called the angry self. They aren't real, but we make them real. By embracing them as part of who we are, we develop power over them and see the truth about them. Then we are free to focus on more important issues and advance to the next level on the spiral of life.

Katy's intention was to help me recognize and embrace various layers of my shadow, rather than to reject or try to repress them. She helped me see them as parts of myself. Once embraced, they would no longer run my life.

Pieces of the Puzzle

Many synchronicities[10] occurred while I was seeing Katy. For example, on three occasions I ran into the sister of a close family friend, George, who had passed away fifteen years before. I had been thinking of him, often feeling his presence, even after all this time had passed. Seeing her so frequently in the course of a few months affirmed to me that George was, indeed, around.

Lithium-free for the first time in months, I could feel emotions again. My body started to lose the spare tire, and gradually, over a period of about four weeks,

---

[10] Synchronicity is a word coined by Carl Jung to describe the coincidences that happen in our lives in a manner that is meaningful to the people experiencing them, and that meaning suggests an underlying pattern. From *Synchronicity* (2006, Sept. 11). *Wikipedia, The Free Encyclopedia*. Retrieved 22:35, Sept. 11, 2006, from www.wikipedia.org

my depression lifted. What an inspiration! I knew this was only the beginning—the best was yet to come.

A Glimpse into the Future

I saw Katy again just before Christmas. The session began as it had each week but soon took a dramatic turn. While on the table, I saw only black and white instead of colors. Katy felt certain this reflected an imminent and significant spiritual shift. During the debriefing, she decided to share an account of her own dramatic transformation.

A couple of years before, during one of Katy's energy sessions, she had seen the Virgin Mary. Katy's spirit left her body and was catapulted to another dimension while her physical body went through a dramatic catharsis. She convulsed, writhed, and gyrated on the table, shouting and shaking. A number of people, including her husband, who was there to support her, had to hold her down, frightening many of the people in the room.

That's pretty incredible, I thought. I didn't judge but listened and agreed that something big might be heading my way. I had no idea what to expect, but I believed that I was going to overcome depression once and for all.

Aware of Lithium's long-term toxic effects on the body, I drank a lot of water and juiced beets and organic greens to speed up the detoxification process. I listened to subliminal tapes, meditated in the morning, journalled, and then listened to the tapes again at night. Each day I prayed for a miraculous breakthrough.

Get Prepared; Get Prepared...

Shortly after Christmas, my friend Marie invited me to dinner at her home with her parents. Again, I felt a connection with her father. He was evolved spiritually and sometimes offered astrological readings for family and special friends. It occurred to me that a reading might help my process. I felt comfortable asking him, but when I did, he became agitated and responded abruptly, "Not tonight." My stomach did a "wee whamp." I knew there was something he wasn't telling me. My stomach always knows.

During dinner, he spoke about something called a Kundalini experience[11]. I listened intently to every word. He had undergone a Kundalini awakening and described it in detail. He didn't know why he was sharing his experience, but he thought I should know.

His instructions were emphatic. If I ever found myself going through a Kundalini rising, I should eat heavy, rich, fatty foods, including meat—all the foods I usually avoided, stop meditating, and allow the energy to flow. I should also refrain from my spiritual practices.

Both stories were very different, yet equally intense, depicting dramatic spiritual breakthroughs. Exactly what was in store for me?

---

[11] Kundalini is seen as energy that usually rests at the base of the spine. When this energy is awakened, it rises slowly up the spinal column to the top of the head. This may mark the beginning of a process of enlightenment. From *Spiritual Emergency: When Personal Transformation Becomes a Crisis*, ed. by Stanislav Grof, MD, and Christine Grof, 1989, p. 101.

Chapter 6:
THE BIG KAHUNA

Over the next few days, my energy increased, my appetite decreased, as did my need for sleep. I worked out at the gym frequently. I felt *free*!

I began to hear the voice of my intuition (my inner guide) in a new way. It grew stronger and clearer. It was like my voice only in a different vibration, a wise, higher being offering loving insight.

I experienced "a-ha" moments, woven together like colorful threads on the tapestry of my own life and about life itself. One day at the gym, for example, I had a conversation with a young woman studying psychotherapy about expansion of consciousness, God, angels, synchronicities, and connecting with people on the same spiritual path. Within minutes, we both felt as if we had known each other for years. Suddenly, we began to experience odd sensations—and I felt like I was no longer standing in the gym on this earth. (I was relieved to find that she had the same experience. Whew!)

My sensations, physical and emotional, intensified. I continued to receive insights, and my awareness increased. Things appeared brighter, crisper, and more alive. I felt an enhanced sense of love, and my energy increased daily. Perhaps this was the result of meditation, exercise, and the continued cleansing/juicing process. The wise inner voice came through with greater clarity.

On New Year's Eve, during a black-tie dinner with Craig and Lynette, the voice within became more amplified. Suddenly, like my skydiving experience, I separated from my physical body. I had to keep refocusing throughout that evening so as not to concern anyone.

The rest of that week, I remained in a heightened state of awareness. I was uncannily psychic, knowing details about people I had just met (such as their birthdates) and having insights about them. I picked up on their thoughts and completed their sentences. I continued to have strong premonitions.

In retrospect, I probably should have kept a lid on some of my insights. For example, while talking to my cousin Jenn, I had revelations and communications from her father, who had passed away years before. Naturally, I felt comfortable sharing my deepest thoughts and excitement about what I was experiencing, but I quickly sensed her fear and uneasiness. She left abruptly, and I knew I had said too much.

The Christmas Tree

Before the season even began, the idea of decorating my Christmas tree had stimulated my creative juices. I bought white lights, white lace, Victorian cherub ornaments, and big crimson ribbons with gold trim. I covered the base of the tree in fine Irish white linen. Everything was new and more elegant and sophisticated than my decorations had ever been.

I loved my tree makeover, and I didn't want to take it down. In fact, the inner voice "told" me to leave it up, so I did. On January 6, it still looked perfect. I was thrilled. It kept the holiday spirit alive.

The Blizzard

The night before the blizzard, while on the phone with a friend, I was overcome with foreboding. I could feel the hair on my arms stand up. I felt someone close to me was going to die. At that moment, one of the three candles I had lit earlier went out.

The next morning, Sunday, January 7, it started snowing. The Blizzard of '96 was on its way. Snow always reminds me of happy childhood memories, the warmth of home, a fire in the fireplace, and the aromas from my mother's baking. It would keep the holiday spirit going and give me another excuse to keep my tree up for a few more days. I lit the tree lights, then called my mother.

I commented that I felt her mother's presence. I was simmering homemade potpourri made with grapefruits and cloves. She said, "That's odd. That's what my mother used to do. It made the house smell great." *Co-inky-dink?* Perhaps…

Feeling excited about the storm was normal, but unusual was my strong urge to clean late at night. I ripped apart closets, purged bookcases, and threw out papers and work materials. The cleaning and purging was cathartic. Everything was organized, clean, and clutter free. I could feel a huge energy shift in my home, and I was relaxed and peaceful.

As I prepared for bed, the voice of my higher self returned with more revelations[12]. I received insight after insight rapidly, as if downloading files from a computer. Some were pieces of information about the past. Some were about the present, and others were visions of the future. Some were about my family, about life—one thought after another, pouring in with incredible rapidity. It was astounding. Smiling, I turned off the lights and got into bed.

Then a tingling started in my left foot, flowing into my stomach. I touched my stomach and felt the vibration. At the same time, I heard a humming sound. A warm, brilliant light streamed down from above and bathed my body. I could see it with my eyes closed. I got up, turned on the lights, and tried to get reoriented by touching things around me. Even with the lights on, I could see and feel that ethereal light above me. Then my whole body started to vibrate intensely.

This was not like anything I had imagined. I knew this was my time, and I trusted myself (thank you Katy). In that instant, I recognized that my prayers for a breakthrough had been answered. Marie's father's words came to me in a flash: "Remember to ground yourself. Eat heavy foods, fats, and meats."

---

[12] **Revelation** is the act of revealing or disclosing, or making something obvious and clearly understood through active or passive communication with the divine. Revelation can originate directly from a deity, or through an agent, such as an angel. Source: www.wikipedia.org

I was too exhilarated to sleep. Outside the window, the blizzard was intensifying. The gusting winds mirrored the flurry of messages I was receiving. I wanted to talk to someone about what was happening, someone who could understand and reassure me. I made several calls to my sister-in-law, Lynette, who had also been in therapy with Sandy. She had been an inspiration during my bouts of depression, and I relied on her a great deal.

On one of those phone calls, I confided that weeks before, I had received strong intuitive impulses to separate spiritually from Craig, my brother (her husband). I relied on him too much. I needed to give him space and freedom to acclimate to their recent marriage. He had taken on a father/husband role with my mother and me, and I wanted to support him and Lynette in starting their own family. She agreed and seemed to understand.

A little later, I spoke to her again. I shared my experience of the vibrations and the insights I was receiving. She claimed she had once had a similar experience and agreed that something special was happening. Her support was a green light for me. I felt delighted and comforted.

Returning to the bedroom, I could see the same pure white light streaming into my body from above. It was so penetrating that it took my breath away. My whole body was filled with love and serenity.

The now familiar inner voice went on. I was given new perspectives on past events. I was told that we each have a mission here. We all choose our lives, and this insight made it easier for me to take responsibility for my choices.

George

At Lynette's suggestion, I began to journal my experience. It was about 3:30 a.m., and the snow was coming down in sheets. I turned on the Christmas tree lights and saw their reflection in the window. From out of nowhere I heard, "PSSSSSSSSSST," and looked around to see where it was coming from. "Who's here?" I wondered aloud. I didn't see anyone, but I could sense the presence of George, a family friend who had died years ago.

I recognized his voice, so I asked, "Where are you?"

"Over here, behind the Christmas tree." Peeking around the tree, I could see a white fuzzy sphere shimmering with its own light. It had a cherub-like aspect. I recognized George immediately.

I asked, "Why aren't you appearing in the body I remember?" He said he was afraid he would scare me. He knew how much I loved the Christmas tree and decided to hide there to surprise me. I began to cry. The tears welled up from deep within and poured out of me. It became clear why I needed to keep the tree up; it was part of the process.

George radiated an image of a loving, smiling, happy, and content spirit. He said he watched over my family, especially my eldest brother, Michael, who was in crisis. George asked me to watch out for him too. I promised.

When George left, I sat down to consider what had happened. Was it real or imagination? Did I really see and speak to the spirit of a dead person? I believe that I did, and George's visit healed something in me. He had spent the last months of his life at Sloan Kettering. I loved him and visited often until he passed away. His death at thirty-nine devastated us all, but I had not fully released my grief until that night.

Peak Experience

My encounter with George assured me that although we must leave the earth plane, we are alive in other dimensions. My beliefs about the afterlife were validated. Yet, what happened next was probably the most profound moment of this entire experience.

I heard the loving inner voice assuring me that I was about to receive an incredible gift, that I was ready to get rid of the dark depression that clung to me. I would be released from the black hole in which I had felt imprisoned for much of my life.

Everything was in motion. The snow outside was falling hard; the Christmas lights were beaming brightly. Ideas and feelings flashed like TV channels-surfing through my consciousness. My senses were heightened.

I recalled my therapist Katy's story of her own dramatic out-of-body experience. I remembered Marie's father's advice to stay grounded in the physical world, so I began to grip my arms and legs and to hold onto furniture, and I forced myself to eat some corn chips, in spite of the fact that I wasn't hungry.

I looked at my cat; he had always been psychically connected to me. If anything dangerous were happening, he would have sensed it. He was fine, so I knew I was okay. I felt safe and loved.

Guided by the voice, I walked to the kitchen. It prompted me to pick up a knife, take it into the bathroom, and place it on the vanity, where it was to remain.

What came next was a true out-of-body experience. I thought, *What now?* At that point, I saw my "light body" step forward so that my physical body was standing just behind it. The voice said, "Before you can get to your true self, you need to release the false, dark selves." I recalled Katy talking about the shadow parts of the psyche and the masks we wear. She said recognizing them was the way to reach the true Self and finally become one with God.

My light body picked up the energy of the knife (physically, the knife didn't move). Then the light body moved the *etheric* knife up under my rib cage below my left breast and into my heart, stabbing upward over and over. (Note: this all happened with my light body, not my actual physical body).

I flashed back to puberty, when I had complained that the growing pains felt as though someone were stabbing me. At that time I had a profound fear of being stabbed, thinking it was one of the most grotesque ways to die. But now I just witnessed the psychic stabbing in amazement. What could this mean?

It sounded as if I were in a wind tunnel, as though my head was outside the window of a speeding car. From the pit of my stomach (my faithful barometer) welled up repressed anger, fear, jealousy, and sadness. It was as if they were being sucked up and out of me into the light. I watched as my light body continued to stab. Thick, heavy blackness poured out like a volcano. I could see it and feel it. (Years later when I saw *The Green Mile*, I was reminded of this during the scene when the psychic giant takes on and then expels another man's disease.)

After the expulsion, the light body laid the energy knife down, and the physical sensations subsided. Then, it stepped back into my physical body, picked up the real knife, and I put it back in the kitchen. That was that.

My head was spinning, but I felt clean, lighter, and freer than I ever had before. I was on a higher plane of spiritual connection and understanding. The black hole of deep, chronic depression had finally been emptied. The emotional darkness that had haunted me for years was gone.

Afterwards, I was exhausted yet so at peace. I curled up to sleep with my cats. As I closed my eyes, the vibrations in my stomach and foot started again, stronger now, and at a different frequency. I have never felt so loved in my entire life.

My cats purred with contentment. I could see a white aura around their bodies. Although I'd never seen an aura before, there is no doubt when you see one. It is distinct and energetically visible. Divine presence filled the room, and I, too, was wrapped in white light. Smiling, I fell asleep.

When I woke the next morning, I felt vibrant, light, alert, and refreshed. In other words, brand new. My first thought was, *Holy shit! What happened last night was real.* Still feeling vibrations in my body, I tried to process what had occurred. The inner voice supported and reassured me. At times I felt like I was in another dimension. I struggled to stay grounded, as elation had me bouncing off the ceiling.

The first person I thought of was my brother Craig, who also suffered from depression. During this Christmas season, it was obvious he was in a bad place, struggling with season-related depression. Innocently, I believed my ineffable transformation would help him move through his pain and suffering. I couldn't wait to share my story with him. After all, I told Craig everything; I trusted him above anyone else. It never occurred to me that I might actually alarm him and others, that they might think I was in some kind of emotional crisis.

As if by design, Craig called that morning and suggested we go out for breakfast. Although eighteen inches of snow had fallen, the roads were passable. I excitedly accepted. I dressed in jeans I hadn't fit into for months, a sweater, and some sexy (for my own benefit) Victoria Secret underwear. My old body was back!

Et Tu, Craig?

Craig arrived shortly, followed closely by my father. I couldn't contain my excitement about what had happened. I was ecstatic and wanted to tell Craig, my best friend, all about it. After all, he and Lynette had been instrumental in building my faith in God in recent years, and we frequently got into philosophical and spiritual discussions. I assumed they would be thrilled with what I was about to tell them.

Looking back, I can still see myself exuberantly re-enacting my transformation as they walked into the living room. Craig nodded a lot, as if he understood what I meant by transformation, out-of-body experiences, and so on. My father just stood there and stared blankly. With great animation I described everything that had happened the night before. And I mean everything!

Even as I spoke, I was still receiving insights. One of the insights was how entangled our family was, like the entwined roots of a tree. To demonstrate, I looped and unrolled some gift wrapping twine between my hands. It became a knotted mass. The twine represented the tangle of personalities and codependency so prevalent in our family. My explanations seemed brilliantly clear to me. Craig and my father looked dumbstruck. To clarify, I became more animated and dramatic.

I recounted the scene with the knife in the bathroom and even reenacted it to the best of my ability. When I said the word *knife* while demonstrating, my brother turned white. I recalled that same look from my cousin Jenn a few days before. Undaunted, I continued my twine example, picking up a knife to cut some of it. Psychically, I saw a red flare shoot out of my brother. He looked aghast. His tone changed, and he sternly told me to put the knife down. I did, without hesitation.

In my euphoria and rapid-fire delivery, I had not taken into account my brother's hearing loss in one ear and that he probably didn't grasp most of what I was saying. Paying attention and acute listening were not his strong points. Up to that moment, I had not realized that my story was frightening him and my father. I wasn't helping; I was scaring my brother away. The greatest experience of my life appeared like a drastic break with reality. His sister had flipped!

Shortly thereafter, the assistant super and porter of my building came to the door. They were my buddies, a second family in some ways, caring for my pets when I was away and watching out for me. I had phoned them earlier and asked them to stop by for their annual Christmas bonus.

My father, who had been quiet until now, jumped up suddenly and asked me what I was doing. Seeing my generous gifts, he said, in front of them, "What are you doing giving that much money away?" I was snapped out of my euphoria long enough to tell him to back off, and I gave my friends their Christmas checks.

After they left, there was lingering discomfort in the room. Craig suggested we go out for breakfast and assured me that everything was okay between us. I gleefully agreed to go. I couldn't think of anything I'd rather do than spend time with Craig. Like an excited child, I wanted to share my exuberance with the world.

For me, breakfast was fun, chatty, and light. After breakfast, we stopped to pick up Lynette, and Craig suggested we see a friend of hers from college. *Sure, why not?* I thought. Feelings of euphoria and divine energy continued to stream through every cell of my body. I felt loved and happy. The world was full of a glowing presence, and I was infused with unconditional love. I had always been safe with my brother and sister-in-law. It was a sunny day, and the blizzard was going into the record books. (Little did I realize, so was I.)

The First Bullet

We arrived at the office of Lynette's friend, Rickey, who happened to be a psychiatrist. I did wonder why we were at his office and not his home. I thought perhaps this was for my father because Craig and I believed he needed psychological help. We had recently made it our mission to help Dad, who had never had counseling in his life. Dad was acting odd that day, agitated and uptight. His speech was rapid and nervous. I couldn't put my finger on it, but Craig had something up his sleeve.

We went into the waiting room and met Rickey's wife. She was wearing a faux tiger coat. Feeling playful,

I asked to try it on, and striding briskly, I gave a few fashion runway turns. Instead of applause, I got raised eyebrows—not that a few looks would stop me. I was still feeling the aftermath of the night before. My social filters had not turned back on yet. I was uninhibited in thought, speech, and action. Craig and I usually acted like juveniles when we were together anyway, so what was the big deal?

I gave back the coat and was led into Rickey's office. I noticed Egyptian tapestries on the divan. I was excited to see them because I had been to Egypt a few years earlier. I examined them while Lynette chatted with Rickey. We all sat down together, my father, Rickey, Craig, Lynette, and I.

Rickey began talking about our family, my parents' troubled marriage and divorce. His intrusive questions surprised me and triggered responses that weren't pretty. In frank terms, I told him I wouldn't be led into those troubled waters, and he had no "fucking" business going there. I was just there to meet one of Lynette's friends. I was *not* there to dissect my family's issues. The session didn't last much longer, and I calmed down.

My father, Craig, and Lynette were shocked. I had never used profanity in front of my father. Okay, I did curse among friends, not that I'm proud of that. But speaking this way released me from any remaining familial bondage, and it felt great. I wanted to let my family see me as I was with friends. No more hiding.

We drove back to Craig and Lynette's apartment. As they were getting drinks, I started to talk to my father. He was clearly upset and nervous. I so wanted to help him. It seemed like I'd spent hours talking with him, believing I could help. I was quite forceful, at times gently shaking him and trying to pass on wisdom I'd learned from The Forum. I asked why he was so upset, but he seemed confused and didn't answer. I thought he was trying to open up but was having trouble. We were, I thought, connecting.

Craig and Lynette were barely there. They were making phone calls and not talking to me at all. It didn't concern me, but I noted it as unusual. Then, Craig announced we were going to St. Francis Hospital, a local psychiatric hospital. I asked if we were going to visit my cousin, who had been there a number of times before. He said no, but we were going to visit someone there. Trusting him, I went.

The Second Bullet

When we arrived, I went into a room with my father, Craig, and a doctor. I felt certain that my father was the reason we were there, and concerned that he might have a melt-down. He seemed so distressed and was getting more uncomfortable. I was worried he would not be able to handle being admitted, given the fact that his sister had been committed and received ECT (electroconvulsive therapy) a number of times. I received clairvoyant information about my father's stress over committing his sister, and it became clear why he felt so out of sorts in this environment. My mind raced. I thought, *How can I help my poor father? I can't let that happen to him!* Thoughts whirled through my mind.

Don't Try This at Home

Then the light bulb went on. I got it! I got it!! A brilliant idea! I would save him. I'd take the attention off of him and put it on me by pretending to have a breakdown. This would bring him back to his senses. The whole family would come together in that crisis. What a plan!

You may well ask, "What were you thinking?" Perhaps I was, at that moment, crazy *not* to think of the consequences of an action like this, yet in my ecstatic state, I couldn't see any danger. Call it poor planning, but I was still in the midst of processing the most unusual spiritual event of my life, and my sense of identity was being radically shifted in the midst of all this.

What I needed that day was a nurturing guide/coach/mentor who understood what I was going through and would support me with acceptance and calm. Too bad that person was nowhere to be found.

I chose my brother Craig as the catalyst for acting out a breakdown. He was always pulling crazy antics in public, in front of us. He had a history of embarrassing us with crude behavior, which at times was not funny. Now it was my turn. I'd get him back for all the times I'd been embarrassed.

I gave a stellar performance, copying everything I could remember that Craig used to entertain us. Uninhibited and willful, I faked picking my nose and flicked it to Craig. I spoke crudely. I crossed my eyes at him and gave him the finger. I babbled like a playful five-year-old, all in front of the doctor and my father. I was funny, childlike, silly, and uninhibited. So I thought.

Looking back now, I believe I was given a chance to release the reserved, quiet little girl who held everything in when she was around her family. I set her free. As crazy as this might have seemed, I believe it was all a necessary part of my kundalini awakening.

As Craig and my father spoke with the doctors, I heard words like "admit" and "how long?" I saw papers on the doctor's desk. Then, as if someone had thrown cold water in my face, I was shocked back into reality. They were committing *me!* My mind flashed back over the entire day: the morning, my father's agitation, the visit to Rickey's office, the phone calls, and now a trip to a mental hospital. Yeow! It hit me like a thunderbolt. This day had been about me, not my father.

Realizing that I had been duped, I went berserk. I walked over to Craig and said, "I can't believe this, you bastard. Fuck you." I said the same to my father. Then I punched my brother in the chest. I was livid. My father and the doctor jumped up. I said, "Is this what happened with Aunt Maria?" I followed up with more choice words, and things quickly heated up. My fate was sealed. I had gone out of control in a nuthouse.

Signed, Sealed, and Delivered

Two security guards came in. I began explaining to them that I had faked acting crazy, but it was too late. A SWAT team of burly male staff members arrived. I was to be escorted out, away from my brother and father.

Of course, I didn't go quietly. I resisted, and the escorts grabbed my arms. I struggled. On went a straitjacket, and I was placed on a gurney. This was not a good thing to do to a pissed-off, defiant woman. Screaming, I was rolled down the hall.

It was bizarre on many levels. I actually recognized one of the staff members wheeling me down the hall. Days earlier I had seen him at the dry cleaners. He said, "Didn't I see you at the cleaners the other day?"

His question helped me snap out of it. I calmed down. I told him I had faked it, and this was a mistake. He didn't seem convinced. Let's face it, who would have believed me at this point?

So I resumed resisting, kicking, screaming, ranting, and raving—just in case my family might still be able to hear me. Through the swinging doors, I shouted, "I'm faking it!"

Chapter 7:
THE QUIET ROOM

I felt disoriented, not sure this was really happening. Perhaps being wheeled down the hall strapped to a gurney in a straitjacket was part of being in an altered state or dream. I needed to get my bearings, so I reassured the staff I had not gone berserk. I told them I was concerned for my father and had acted crazy to take the attention off him. What a sacrifice I had made! "Yeah, sure," I heard as I was wheeled into the holding area to The Quiet Room.

While in the holding area, one of the escorts transmogrified into Sandy, my former therapist. I screamed, "Oh my God, Sandy!" at the confused staff member. Suddenly, as if I were opening files on a computer, I was able to recall and process the work I had done with him. I don't know what the staff member thought, but seeing Sandy in front of me was as clear as the light of day. My kundalini shift was still going on as I shuttled between my earthly existence and an altered consciousness.

Suddenly, I was rolled off the gurney onto a mattress. Then, without seeing my medical records or asking about sensitivity to drugs or allergies, I was held down, my pants were pulled down, and I was given a shot in the butt with a huge needle. A number of the staff looked on, suppressing smiles and joking. Although I was still in a heightened spiritual state, this shocked me back into their reality, where I was bewildered and not able to fully comprehend what was going on. How could something so blessed and transforming turn so quickly into a catastrophe?

Furious and humiliated, I fought, cursed, and screamed, demanding to know what they had given me. There was no reply. Livid, I was determined not to allow my body to be affected by the drugs. I focused all my attention inward, praying that the effects would be negated.

Soon after, the straitjacket was removed. More horse-sized injections were administered without my consent. Naturally, I resisted and cursed. The staff dragged me into The Quiet Room, a closely supervised twenty-four-hour area for newly arrived patients or badly behaved ones (I was both). I was forced to lie face down on the bed, and my arms and legs were strapped tightly to the corner posts. The staff had no qualms about kneeing me in my already injured back or using force to keep me under control. The pain and humiliation enraged me. I went ballistic.

After what seemed like hours of screaming at the inhumanity of my situation, I gave up, more due to a sore throat and sheer physical exhaustion. Yikes! It hit me. I was trapped inside a mental institution.

Crucifixion

Four-point restraint was physically painful. The leather straps were pulled so tight that I was bruised and raw on both wrists and ankles, more from struggling than anything. My neck became stiff, and my back ached terribly.

As I lay there, a profound insight came upon me. I was reminded of the crucifixion of Christ. My thoughts went to the pain and humiliation Christ must have endured. Lying face down, arms and legs stretched excruciatingly, I got a glimpse of what he might have felt.

It was primitive and inhumane. There was no one to comfort or listen to me. I felt total dejection. I will *never* forget that experience!

Then, the wise, loving voice prodded me to look around the room. Pictures were painted on the walls. Overhead, I could just see one of a little girl with a long ponytail. I related to her as a younger image of myself. Across the room were Rorschach animals ranging from a rabbit to an elephant. I turned my stiffened neck to view the entire room as best I could. Meticulously printed in tiny letters on the wall near my head was, "Love the one you're with." This note from a fellow sufferer filled me with serenity. The voice spoke again, "You will be guided through this crisis." I wasn't crazy. God was with me and had been all along. Even this was a true blessing.

The restraints were no longer my enemy. Now, I was certain I would survive anything. My prayers and connection to God would carry me through. Hours later, I was taken out of the restraints and fell into a dreamless sleep.

Getting to Know You

As I awoke the next morning, I met Roxie, the nurse's aide, an African-American woman I connected with immediately. She was God-sent. She became my confidante and cheerleader. She believed in me. I could trust her. I told her my story, and she was a real grounding force.

It quickly became clear to the staff that I would be no ordinary Quiet Room patient. First of all, the rooms were filthy and unfit even for an animal. *How funny*, I thought, *that when people believe your mind goes, they think you can live in deplorable conditions.* In the communal bathroom, the shower had old, used soap congealed on the floor. Mildew and foul odors pervaded the toilet area. The upholstery had urine and feces stains from previous patients. I wanted to vomit from the conditions. Disgusted, I complained to the staff, demanding that the rooms be cleaned up. I threatened to report the hospital for infestation of bacteria and disease. "Crazy or not," I said, "this is a hospital."

Badgering worked. The staff responded by sending in Maria, a member of the janitorial staff. Maria understood little English, so I spoke to her in Spanish about cleaning and disinfecting the area, especially the bathroom, and changing my sheets every day. She seemed puzzled by my request but followed my instructions.

Day One

The interrogation began. A psychiatrist came to my room, pen in hand, prepared to medicate. After all, this was a drug-based institution, I mean, psychiatric hospital. The doctor remarked, "You're bipolar and had a manic episode." It was an indictment, not a diagnosis, which I rejected immediately. Just as quickly, I dismissed him.

That day I told my version of what happened to three different doctors, all of whom were unwilling to listen to my story of spiritual transformation. They had no interest in hearing me. Counseling was out of the question while I was the Quiet Room; medication was my only option. I refused to allow any of those doctors to see me again.

Then, Dr. Horowitz, Chief of Psychiatry, came in and announced that he was taking over my case since I had found the rest of the staff unfit. Dr. Horowitz was tall and thin with receding hair, thick glasses, and a prominent nose. Something about him made me sick. I soon learned what.

He began, "I understand you've had a bipolar episode and need to be medicated." His voice was pompous and detached. His bedside manner was cold as he read the chart. His diagnosis was mania; the treatment was drugs.

Property of the State

I pleaded with Dr. Horowitz. I did not need medication, nor did I want it. I had successfully detoxified my body from the effects of Lithium, and I was determined to remain that way. I pointed out that the information from Rickey and my family the day before did not take into account my spiritual experience.

Dr. Horowitz stood with arms crossed. He refused to make eye contact. I got a lot of uh-huhs and um-hums. At last, he responded, "Your hyper-religiosity is a typical part of a manic episode. You need medication." My story meant zip, zero, nada!

Now I was really pissed. I refused to consent to being drugged. He informed me that I would be taken to court by the hospital to assess my competency. He threatened even bigger guns than Lithium. I let him have both barrels of my frustration and fury.

The Cuckoo's Nest

The meeting with Dr. Horowitz stunned me. This was something out of a movie—the classic case of the misunderstood patient done in by her doctor, family, and society. The unthinkable was happening, but my imagination teased me with a vision of what a movie this would make. I began to journal (yes, I was allowed pencil and paper).

In the movie, *Harvey*, Jimmy Stewart, as the socially irresponsible Elwood P. Dowd, was committed to a mental hospital, but his sister relented and came back just in time to save him. At this point, however, my future looked bleak. Trying to convince these people that I had not had a manic episode was futile. Refusing medication might not be possible. I was stuck in their world and apparently I was not going to get out any time soon.

Staying angry didn't fit someone who had sought and gone through the life-altering event I had experienced, but squelching my emotions was not an option either. There was no going back. The proverbial cork had popped, and it was time to party!

So I let the fun begin. Acting crazier than crazy was the plan, and my Quiet Room was the perfect stage. It was 8 x 10 feet and encased in glass almost from floor to ceiling. Staff could see me from their offices at any time. There was twenty-four-hour surveillance.

Working the System

To regain some power, I'd do my best to turn the tables on the staff. A little reverse psychology would be fun. The three steps of Plan A were:

1. Room Service
2. Private Time
3. Redecorate

I turned twenty-four-hour surveillance into "twenty-four-hour room service." I wanted privacy but also lots of attention. Second, I would remain in the Quiet Room indefinitely to use the private time to process all that had happened. Finally, I'd redecorate the living area so it would at least be tolerable.

The Quiet Room was considered a temporary holding area for patients who were out of control, had injured themselves, or were likely to hang themselves. Most entered the Quiet Room in four-point restraints and were pumped full of serious drugs. The shots often made them delirious, causing vomiting and the runs. Typically, they would be returned to their regular floor the next day.

Life on the floor, however, was dramatically different. It was regimented, with programs scheduled all day. Out there, I would not be allowed to process my transformation quietly. Staying in the Quiet Room could help me focus within. The Quiet Room actually became somewhat of a sanctuary.

Oh yes, they were still watching me, but I made the 24/7 attention work for me. I loved annoying them; the more I could interrupt them, the better. I would badger, complain, and order things whenever I could. Maria cleaned the bathroom and changed my sheets every day. I used the extra sheets to drape the tables and chairs, hiding the filth and stains. I knotted the sheets into bows on the corners so they looked pretty. I colored and drew on the white tray mats with the four crayons provided by staff. I put flowers on the table during dinner. These simple changes made for a livable space. It was empowering. The staff tried to interfere, but I insisted, resisted, and persisted until I got my way.

Not having access to clothes, makeup, or toiletries, I felt pretty gross. The hospital provided putrid-smelling castile soap. I took showers holding my breath or breathing through my mouth to avoid the smell. Thinking of my mother, the seamstress, I redesigned the hospital-issued pajamas. One day I'd make a midriff-baring shirt (oops, manic behavior—exposing the body); the next, workout shorts requiring just a rip here and there and rolling up the sleeves (another real no-no). The hospital gowns weren't DKNY, but it was a start. Anything to avoid looking like a patient! Anything to show them I was okay.

My hair, however, remained a problem. Without a blow dryer or hair products, I was on serious hair alert. My solution was only a patient away. Delia, a patient who refused her meds, was brought into the Quiet Room area with me. She was a young, attractive African-American and was using a hospital towel as a turban. I thought, *How clever! What a great way to get rid of bedhead.* I asked her to show me how to wrap a turban for myself. (Chad, a staff aide and spy for the therapists, told me later that the turban was noted as a clear indicator of ongoing manic behavior.)

Richard Simmons, Eat Your Heart Out

I had to return to a daily exercise routine! I needed to work out. The problem was a lack of equipment, so I had to be creative. I used a shower stool as a modified step and began an aerobics workout. It would have been nice to have a Richard Simmons video.

My routine was quickly cut short by Dr. Horowitz, who ordered me to stop all exercise at once. He said it made me too animated, and left. After that, I tried to sneak exercise into ordinary activity, but it wasn't worth it.

Family Circus

My brothers (minus Michael), mother, and father came to visit soon after I was admitted. Craig was first, along with my father. I refused to speak, telling them to leave. I had nothing to say to them.

My mother returned with Brad the next day. She made a dramatic entrance, wearing an amber fox coat and one of her many St. John knits as if she were about to step onto a fashion runway. She seemed happy to see me. I tried to explain the confusion—that I had not really had a breakdown. It didn't take long to realize she was placating me. Tearfully, she said, "I spoke to the doctors, and they think you should be medicated." Even though she knew how much I wanted to avoid drugs, how much I was against drug therapy, she still accepted the doctors' treatment plan over mine.

As if I had taken a dose of truth serum, I let my resentment and feelings of betrayal be known. Both left shortly thereafter.

Restrained Again

During the day, I was able to visit the staff area and make requests for phone calls. The staff area was easily accessible to the Quiet Room. While making one of my few phone calls, I was told that my time was up. My response was rather sassy, and it prompted several staff members to grab and force me back into the Quiet Room. I screamed, "Don't touch me. Watch out for my bad back." Paying no attention, the staff shoved and pushed. As I struggled, an alarm sounded, and I was again placed in four-point restraint.

It was easier the second time. Once restrained, I didn't resist. There was a two-hour minimum for this punishment, and a black mark went on my record. The incident showed I was still manic.

New in Town?

New patients were a curiosity to everyone on the floor; they were entertainment to break up the monotony. As the new girl in town, I attracted lots of attention.

Word on the floor was that I was trouble, the kind of trouble that patients loved but staff hated. Naturally, those who heard about me wanted to check me out, but the corridor between the Quiet Room and the staff viewing area was off limits. However, there was a small area where patients could get a sneak peek and still be out of view of the staff. Through the thick glass, with sign language and passing notes, we established communication.

Monkey See, Monkey Do

The first few days, patients showed up regularly, staring, rarely speaking. I thought it was pretty rude to view me like a monkey at the zoo, so I decided to give them something to stare at. While I was at it, I might as well add a few more days in the Quiet Room—whatever it took to stay off the floor and keep some semblance of privacy.

The show began. I pretended to swing from chair to chair, jumping around, scratching, and making monkey sounds (you know the ones). I encouraged patients to bang on the glass with me and kept them entertained. I got into the role, and the patients had fun. They called others, and a little crowd gathered. The perplexed staff heard banging and entered the room. They insisted that I stop, and I was reprimanded. Of course, this meant extended time in the Quiet Room. Mission accomplished!

There was a catch, however, to remaining in the Quiet Room, which I didn't figure out for some time. The longer your stay there, the longer your overall stay in the hospital. Protocol dictated that a patient must remain on the floor and out of the Quiet Room for a specified number of days before release could be considered. Although I thought of it as my safe haven, I was nowhere near being considered for release.

Fashion Makeover for Phil

The monkey business incident broke the ice with the other patients. One patient I remember in particular approached the window demurely. He was unkempt, unshaven, and unclean. His greasy hair had not been combed or cut in months. What a mess! And he was obviously heavily medicated.

He seemed intrigued with me, so I approached and signaled through the glass. I articulated carefully, and said, "You're a good-looking guy, but you need to wash your hair." An hour later, he returned with his hair washed. Then I said, "Phil, you'd look really good if you cut your hair." The next day, he appeared with a haircut. "Phil, take a shower. Change your clothes," I said. The next day he returned showered with clean clothes. Over several days, I orchestrated his personal makeover. In just a few days, he was outwardly transformed, and his demeanor changed. He was walking with animation and more confidence. He was even smiling!

Week Two: Life on the Farm

I remained in control of the Quiet Room for an entire week. By now, I was starting to get used to visitors. They came in five flavors: patients, staff, phone calls, friends, and family.

At the beginning of the second week, a social worker came to visit. She was assigned to be my representative to the court concerning my refusal to be medicated. I related my story again, but her interest seemed, at best, polite. I understood from her that the hospital would try to get a court order to medicate me and prove I was incompetent to make decisions for myself. I would appear with her at the hearing to dispute this. I was not convinced that this woman believed me or that she would truly represent me, although I had made what I wanted very clear. The future looked grim.

Suddenly, it became clear that my incarceration had a purpose. I could get out of here and write a book, make a movie, take a stand for changing the system. Perhaps these were grandiose ideas, but this was a problem that had to be exposed. Somebody had to do something!

Close Encounters

By this time, my room was clean and decorated-vastly improved. I was able to draw, have time to myself, and communicate with others. It wasn't so bad. In comparison with the rest of the hospital, The Quiet Room was a retreat.

This fact didn't go unnoticed. A few women from the floor actually faked acting out so they could join me. They said I seemed way too content and was getting an incredible amount of attention. They wanted in on it. They made a good point.

Although you might have thought that relinquishing my privacy bothered me, it didn't. Just the opposite! These extraordinary women opened my eyes and expanded my views on the typical mental patient. Yes, they struggled with depression, anger, and personal issues. However, I was astounded to see that they were also intelligent, interesting, creative, artistic, accomplished, and remarkable. They gave me the gift of appreciation. We really enjoyed each other's company.

Margaret

I felt I could help other patients who came to the Quiet Room. Margaret was an educated professional in an executive position, but she was clinically depressed and had suicidal thoughts. Although she was bright, articulate, and poised, she was notorious for repeating the same thing over and over, and she tried to convince me that she had no control over any of it.

Looking for the positive, I spent hours with her sharing my story and listening to hers, hoping to give her a more positive view of herself. I started coaching her to stop playing the victim role, to celebrate the incredible talents she had, and to take charge of her life.

Chloe

Chloe, in her twenties, was a long-termer who used suicide attempts to remain institutionalized. Afraid to return to life on the outside, she was using the hospital as a safety net. She was placed in the Quiet Room for a fake suicide attempt.

Chloe was a trip. She had pierced just about every part of her body, yet she was spiritually wise beyond her years, a brilliant conversationalist, and hilarious. Behind our differences, I recognized a kindred spirit.

Hello, It's Me

The first person I called on the pay phone was my building superintendent, Bill. Bill was more than the super, he was a dear friend and confidante. He was about my father's age but was nothing like my father. He worked with Joseph, a quiet man with an ever-present smile and a heart of gold. I called to tell them what had happened.

Bill thought I was joking at first. Not for a moment would he believe that I should be in the hospital. He was outraged. I asked him not to let anybody in my apartment, and I gave him the phone number of the public phone at the hospital. From then on, he and Joseph called every day. What a blessing! They were such a source of strength and support during this time—they believed me.

I called my college roommate, Jeanie, a social worker in mental health. When I told her about my predicament, she was livid and promised to help me get released. I hung up, grateful to have such a friend. I hadn't seen her in years, but she came to visit the day I called. I remember seeing her through the glass of the Quiet Room. She moseyed on in as if it were no big deal. Her first comment was, "What the hell are you doing in here?" Words couldn't express my gratitude and appreciation. She never looked skeptical. There was no judgment. My faith that I could get out was restored. Jeanie was a ray of sunshine, a lifesaver.

I even continued to work with clients via the pay phone, telling them I was on personal leave. My mind was incredibly clear, and I was able to remember details and requests that had been made weeks ago without referring to any written records.

However, when I attempted to retrieve my phone messages from home, my line had been disconnected. My credit cards were also suspended. My family was behind all this, and it enraged me.

Family Visits: The Eye of the Storm

Conchetta kept showing up, but she never asked about my needs, never offered to bring food. At any other time, my mother would feed me first and ask questions later. Finally, at my request, she did bring in lavender oil. What a relief! Now I could mask the horrific smells. The other patients loved it too. Lavender's fragrance is calming and relaxing, and it seemed to transform the entire floor.

My father visited almost every day—not a good thing. He was certain I had suffered a breakdown, but he told me what I wanted to hear. He had little understanding of spirituality, and to my frustration, what I tried to tell him went right over his head. If I talked of connecting to my higher self (or God), he interpreted it as my entry into a convent. I had to laugh.

Although my brother Brad and I had not spent much time together over the past few years, he was the one who took control. He visited and called frequently. He listened and empathized. He was the only family member to make any attempt to comprehend what was happening to me. This was what I needed, so I thought.

Brad let me know that the *entire* family was meeting together for counseling. Yes, the dream my brother Craig and I shared was at last achieved—the entire family was united around one issue. It had been years in the making—it just hadn't played out the way I had thought it would.

Pushing Pills: To Medicate or Not to Medicate

In the middle of my second week, I was to appear in court. The judge would determine if medication was necessary. The social worker was to be my advocate. Brad had said he would appear to support my no-drug stance, but the day before, he called and backed out. He said he was afraid to take on this responsibility. He just couldn't do it. Thank you, Brad!

That was the last straw. My family had put me in a mental hospital; I didn't go voluntarily. Now Brad was having a meltdown. What did he expect me to do? I had been tricked by my brother, father, and sister-in-law, put in a straitjacket, drugged up with Lord knows what and physically abused. Okay, I would get out of this without them. I would appear in court by myself.

The next morning, before I left to appear in court, Delia arrived back in the Quiet Room. She fought with the staff not to drug her, not to harass her, and to leave her alone. Still furious over Brad's betrayal, I began to yell suggestions through the wall to Delia, like "Don't let them drug you. Stand your ground." Then I became abusive with the staff, cursing and calling them names. They soon had enough and placed me in four-point restraints for the third time and drugged me again against my will. The court was notified that I had acted out and was uncontrollable. My fate was sealed. I would not be allowed to appear in court.

Enter Dr. Horowitz. He had been made aware of my family situation, my anger at the staff, and my lack of control when Delia was brought in. He informed me that, like it or not, I would begin drug therapy immediately. Believing I would refuse pills, he prescribed a liquid drug to be administered by the staff and monitored with blood tests. I would be allowed to choose my poison. The pickings were slim. If I didn't agree to something, he would put me on Thorazine. I knew this medication would literally knock the life out of me and glaze me over like most of the patients at St. Francis. Depakote, his second choice, was also a heavy gun.

I tried to explain one last time. My passionate pleas only served to confirm his diagnosis—manic. My anger escalated; I was not being heard. *One Flew Over the Cuckoo's Nest* made exquisite sense: outraged patients trapped as victims of the system, forced into a situation where disagreement only validates the diagnosis. Depakote would begin the next day.

Drugs

The next day, Dr. Horowitz and his staff were eager for me "to reach therapeutic levels as quickly as possible," meaning they wanted me to feel the effects of Depakote quickly. I complained that they were giving too high a dose too fast, to no avail. This dose would allow the staff to handle me better.

The side-effects came quickly: abdominal pain, diarrhea, nausea, headaches; I was wiped out and hated knowing my body was being violated with a toxic medication. I couldn't bear the thought of taking one more dose. I had to find a way *not* to take my meds. I needed a new plan and fast.

Medications were administered after dinner, during quiet time, when everyone had to relax in their rooms. The staff teamed up when it came time to administer my meds. I pretended to be sound asleep. The drug was supposed to calm me. It was expected that I'd slow down. When Suzie (the Nurse Ratchet of St. Francis) and her assistant announced themselves, the show began.

She literally shook me awake. (I recalled my brother Larry faking sleeping as a kid while my mother shook him.) It took everything in me not to laugh. Suzie suspected I was faking it. Now I had to get into the role.

I acted groggy, as if I were really out of it. I told her I couldn't bear taking any more medication, that I was nauseous and would most definitely get sick if she pushed me. I couldn't have been clearer.

I took the medicine cupful of liquid and swallowed, paused a second, and straight-faced spit it out as if I were vomiting. It went all over her face and dripped down her chest. She was livid! She threatened to report me to Dr. Horowitz, which could mean even more medication. I had to bite my tongue not to laugh. Quickly, I reverted to crying, convincing her I really was sick and apologizing profusely, begging Suzie not to tell Dr. Horowitz. She relented and left. I laughed so hard my sides hurt.

As the days passed, Depakote reached therapeutic levels, and the side effects decreased. As the diarrhea and nausea lessened, my energy level rose. Within a few days, I felt like myself again. I was warned by my peers to calm down and watch myself, or Dr. Horowitz would surely add another drug.

All the World's a Stage

I began to write notes on the back of the paper mats provided during lunch in the Quiet Room. I documented the insane behavior of the staff. Roxie, the nurse's aide who cared for me, told me some of the regulations at St. Francis. I jotted them down on the paper mats, ever aware that any sign of assertion, outspokenness, or energy would be interpreted as mania and reported by staff. This was the hardest part, squelching my normally passionate and expressive nature.

One nurse in particular, Marrea, would come into my room every evening and, in a saccharine-tone voice, ask, "Is everything okay? Are you in controls?" It took everything for me not to react to her prodding. After several nights, I reported her. My complaints fell on deaf ears.

Phoning Home

I refused to take Brad's calls for a few days but finally relented. Based on meetings with Dr. Horowitz, Brad insisted that my only way out of the hospital was to agree to medication. I would have to placate the staff by, in essence, agreeing with their diagnosis. In other words, lie. Since it was up to Horowitz to decide my fate, I had to play the game—his game. From the staff's point of view, medication was the only answer. To them, my behavior indicated a manic episode. End of story. Period. I had to accept that. And then the kickers—I'd have to reconnect with my family and get out of the Quiet Room quickly. Those were the conditions under which I could get released. This was sobering news.

I immediately began behaving better toward the staff, and I stopped all my schemes. At the beginning of the third week, Dr. Horowitz released me from the Quiet Room.

Chapter 8:
OUT OF THE FRYING PAN

The Floor

My stomach churned at the thought of leaving the Quiet Room. I had enjoyed the so-called privacy; at least I had alone time. The twenty-four-hour monitoring seemed less offensive than having to participate in scheduled activities *out on the floor*. The floor did have some advantages. It was less restrictive, there was no twenty-four-hour supervision, and I could use knives and forks when eating.

As I expected, the most difficult change was the daily mandatory activities beginning at 9:00 a.m. and going until 4:00 p.m. There might be an hour of group therapy, then a workshop, then perhaps a lecture on some sort of therapy. It was like going back to high school, only worse!

Floor Mates

Surprisingly, I bonded quickly with the other patients, who banded together for the purpose of outsmarting the staff. Most of them already knew who I was by the time I got on the floor. They were intrigued and wanted to know why (and how) I had stayed in the Quiet Room for such a long time. Many commented that I sounded articulate, coherent, and alert. They couldn't understand why I had been hospitalized in the first place. It felt good to be regarded that way.

They coached me on how to act and how *not* to act on the floor.
1. No horseplay of any kind.
2. No signs of being energetic; act like a zombie.
3. Act dead.

Breaking any of these rules resulted in higher doses of medication or an extended stay. After hearing the rules, I thought, *Now you tell me who the nuts are!*

A Fine Line

Many patients spoke of their strong spiritual beliefs. Many were alcoholics or drug abusers with significant emotional issues. I believe they were caught in-between worlds. For whatever reasons, they were unable to live in the present. They were not grounded, or they existed in a reality beyond this one. They were confused and unable to choose one world over the other.

Having just experienced my own separation of self and altered states of consciousness, I empathized with them. (In fact, that may have been part of the learning I was to do here.) I was fortunate to have been guided by my higher self, and I had learned from therapists and friends how to ground myself and process my experience. It was clear to me that these individuals, some with amazing stories, had no tools, no one to take them seriously, and no way to get help in this hospital. God only knows what their medications did to them. I felt that I had to try to help.

The patients sensed that something special had happened to me. Some said they could see an aura around me, that I was glowing or surrounded by white light. Others came up to touch me and ask if I was physically real; one thought I might be an angel.

I was touched by their sensitivity and believed they might benefit from hearing about my experience. I spoke from my heart, and they seemed to appreciate that. I began telling my story and often had a group of patients listening and sharing their experiences, and wanting to know more. We were captivated.

Telling my story kept it alive and validated its meaning: I did have a true spiritual awakening. Connecting to these people, I had a profound realization that I was among like-minded individuals, not insane people. My beliefs about so-called mentally ill people were radically changed. If I were caught in the system, and they were caught in the system, how many thousands of others were caught in a system that didn't understand? I wanted to do something to change this.

For starters, I used my medical background to explain hospital protocol, the latest ups and downs in the pharmaceutical industry, and the pros and cons of using prescription drugs. I began speaking to them about their options to medicate and about the possibility of discharge. To many I offered a different point of view, perhaps, one they had never heard before.

Often I encouraged them to consider stopping the medication that kept them lifeless, glazed over, or made them sleep. I told them that even though patients were required to receive medications by the hospital and the state, they had a right to say no or to inquire about the medications they were taking. Forcing them to take meds, I reminded them, is abusive and unconstitutional (obviously, this was still a major sore point for me).

The staff saw that I was getting attention and counseling many of the patients. I don't think they quite knew what to make of it, but they began to try to use me as a liaison between them and the patients. I remained focused on helping my peers and making the best of the situation. Time for buttering up the staff would come later.

Larissa, My Sidekick

Lunch became a favorite time. We all enjoyed hearing stories during lunch. It was there I befriended Larissa, a brilliant and beautiful seventeen-year-old who had also been hospitalized for manic behavior. Larissa and I clicked immediately. She was bright, spiritual, playful, and most definitely a rebel. What a pair! We played off each other, becoming the center of attention.

Our first lunch together altered the robotic lunchtime routine. Part of our mission was to cheer everyone up. To pick up the tempo, we passed around whatever food or drinks we wanted to trade. Even the despondent patients got involved. Lunchtime became something we all eagerly anticipated.

Larissa and I hung out in each other's rooms, and at night about ten of us would gather until lights out. We engaged in personal conversations and communicated in a loving and supportive manner. Everyone felt safe and accepted. Some were interested in joining us for morning prayers. This experience of holy community was sublime.

At the break of dawn, Larissa and a few others joined me for morning prayers and meditation in my room. We could see a little of the outside world from my window, and the sunrise gave us hope and promised better things to come. In the distance we witnessed one of God's miracles, a speck of orange that would rise above the pinkish blue horizon and blind us with the light. We sat in silence to connect to each other, with our higher power, and God.

Moments like these made my stay in the hospital bearable. My head spun with the profundity of it. It reassured me that this was all supposed to happen. Not only was I still processing my own personal transformation, I was also contributing to and supporting others in their spiritual process. Never in my life have I felt so needed or so useful in contributing to others' well-being.

I began to see St. Francis Hospital as one of the greatest internships of my life. Where else could I have had this experience? Patients came to me for advice and to be heard. I was right where I needed to be.

Arts and Crafts: How Old Are We, Now?

Nurse Suzie, the recipient of my "throwing up" in the Quiet Room, approached me to spearhead the Valentine's Day craft project. Suzie thought if anyone could get the patients together, I could. I agreed. The assignment was to make a huge banner. Everyone was to work on it that afternoon. It would be hung in the entranceway of the floor for visitors to see.

Within a half hour, Larissa and I had even the most difficult patients joining in—even Tim, who had tripped one too many times on acid. The childish arts and crafts assignment actually turned into a significant bonding session for all of us. Reclusive or difficult patients drifted in and quietly drew something that was profound for them. Many contributed words that revealed what was hidden in their hearts.

The completed banner was twenty feet in length and included special phrases, poignant sayings, poetry, and artwork. We enjoyed doing it. The staff was shocked to see that we not only completed it but went beyond our allotted time. A gold star for me! I was moved up into the "maybe she's getting better" category. Go figure!

Mental Illness or Spiritual Emergence?

As the days passed, I was awakened to the fact that many, if not all, of these patients were undergoing some degree of spiritual crisis. Some had experiences similar to mine but had little understanding as to what had occurred. They had not had the benefit of alternative therapists and counselors. Many were victims of a one-track mind and had never ventured beyond psychiatric evaluations, labels, and medications.

It was my pleasure and joy to open a window of hope for them. Some required encouragement. A simple phrase, "Maybe you're not sick," would often lift them. Others needed grounding: to be shown how to stay focused on the here and now. Some needed to know there might be a solution, that someone might take them seriously and help or even cure them. They needed to believe in themselves. Still others needed to talk and be heard. They would come to my room to tell the story of their crises or experiences. They had seen the hand of God in their lives and could count so many blessings. Like me, they needed someone who could understand and believe in them.

To say I had newly acquired talents would be an understatement. I was more vibrant and creative than I have ever been. My mind seemed to have become an encyclopedia of information, one of many positive side effects of the kundalini rising. I didn't know where some of the information was coming from, but it rolled off my tongue. I wrote poetry, produced drawings that exceeded my past abilities, and started on my screenplay. Although I had no prior interest or talent for poetry, drawing, or writing, I was compelled to do it all.

I was still receiving psychic insights, often astounding patients with my uncanny knowledge about them or others. These were not coincidences and not limited to patients. For example, Dr. Horowitz had changed his surname years before and had told no one. When we were introduced, I repeated back his first name and his prior last name. He turned white. How could I know that?

Bless Me, Father?

My attempts to discuss spiritual matters with clergy at the hospital were dismissed. It was ironic that no one in this Catholic hospital accepted the possibility of patients having a personal experience of the divine. Spiritual transformation was synonymous with being crazy, manic, or hyper-religious, a textbook psychiatric viewpoint.

Even in the short time I was in the hospital, it became undeniably clear that patients needed spiritual as well as psychological healing. Clergy represented the possibility for the integration of the two, and yet, they seemed to have no skill or interest. They, like the psychiatric staff, were miserably limited in their understanding of the patients. What opportunities they missed!

Lesson Learned

There are many ineffable parts to a kundalini/spiritual emergence. The hospital was part of the experience, for it was life-changing. But the real change went much deeper. I could never again doubt there was more to me than the exterior Lauren everyone knew. There was a wiser version of me, a higher self that was connecting with the outer me all the time. This part of me was clearly delineated; I could see and hear it. Never again would I question its existence. I know we each have to experience our own connection to our higher selves, but I will forever be aware of this partnership. Perhaps hospitalization gave me the perfect chance to accept and try out this connection.

In the end, I accepted that I would never receive validation from clergy, staff, or family while I was in the hospital. Thank God, I no longer needed it. It was enough that this pivotal, transformational time in my life had been guided and validated by my higher self and many of my friends at the hospital.

Chapter 9:
INTO THE FIRE

Janet and the Gang

Everyone on the floor was assigned a roommate. In my case, I got several—in one. As I was unpacking, Nurse Fanny said, "Oh, by the way, you should know a few things about your new roommate." Janet, I was warned, was a bit difficult, an MPD (multi-personality disorder) patient. Janet had *alters* (other personalities) who exhibited behavior few other patients could handle. "If anyone can deal with Janet," Nurse Fanny said, "you can." I was given these instructions: 1) do not address her alters and 2) report to the staff about her. "We feel she'll do well with you," said the staff. Just kick me!

I met Janet later that afternoon. She had a warm and gentle nature. She was about thirty years old, a registered nurse, and an advanced kung fu student. I would never have guessed her underlying condition.

Later that night, after dinner and visits with Larissa and peers, I came back to my room. There I heard the story of Janet's life. As we were preparing to go to sleep, I asked Janet what the trigger was for her to move into altered states and what would happen while she was there. Janet's story was horrific, but she was articulate and calm. It was difficult to listen to the atrocities visited on her during childhood: parental satanic worship, incest, molestation, and body mutilation. Much worse, the satanic worship involved human sacrifice. She had witnessed people actually killed on an altar.

Yet, it was as if she were speaking about a third party. She seemed to understand her illness and her process clearly. Janet explained that the other personalities saved her during these experiences. She created them to survive on both a physical and mental level. She mentioned the name of one of her favorite alters, Tommy, whom she really loved. He was kind, gentle, and loving.

She spoke so compellingly, there was no doubt in my mind that her story was true. Still I thought, *This is the stuff horror movies are made of!* We spoke late into the night. Janet feared the dark and had problems sleeping. Ya think?

At some point, I went to the bathroom. When I returned, Janet was huddled on the floor in the corner of the room under a blanket. I called to her, asking what was wrong. After I called a number of times, a child's voice responded, "I'm not Janet. I'm Tommy."

Knowing about Tommy ahead of time did not prepare me for the shock of meeting him. I suppose there's no way to prepare for what I was about to experience. My instincts prompted me to speak with Janet through her alter Tommy, contradicting the staff's request not to.

The first thing I asked Tommy was why he was under a blanket. "I'm afraid of the dark," he answered. I was able to help him relax by talking to him. I asked about his likes and dislikes. Soon he began to write, draw, and play like a five-year old. It was remarkable. I prayed and did a meditation with Tommy to ground him and have him connect to the good and loving light around and within him. To the best of my ability, I showed him how to visualize bringing light into his body. He was much calmer at the end of the exercise. I reminded him that he could always use light when he went into dark and scary places. We stayed up until the first light of dawn.

As if with the flip of a switch, when the sun began to rise, Janet returned. She was so thankful for my support and for staying up with Tommy during the night. "Tommy is terribly afraid of the dark," she said. What an understatement.

The next day, staff members reminded me how sick Janet was, claiming her stories were all made up. I could only think, *You guys give "sick" a whole new meaning.* It was hard to imagine that no one on the staff believed her, but this was an all-too-common experience. We were ignored, denied, and disbelieved on a regular basis. I could really identify with Janet!

The days and nights that followed were beyond anything I have seen or read about. Janet had sixteen different personalities, and I met several of them. Some were nice, some were wicked, and some tried to physically injure her.

By far the worst triggers of these alters were the weekly visits from her father (her molester). Believe it or not, her father, who had continued his incestuous relationship with her into adolescence, was allowed to visit weekly. After a visit with her father, one of Janet's violent alters emerged, and she stabbed herself repeatedly with a plastic knife. I was frightened and repulsed. She was immediately restrained and carried to the Quiet Room.

Group B

As I had suspected, being out of the Quiet Room was a hard adjustment. The only thing keeping me in line was my goal—to be released.

I was assigned to Group B, complete with predictably boring sessions for patient education. Less predictable but infuriating was the blatant indoctrination of patients to use pharmaceuticals. We were told that every one of us had a mental illness. Our conditions were diagnosed and labeled, and the only solution was medication.

One afternoon, my group watched a video on depression, sponsored and produced by a major pharmaceutical company. Hello? Is there anything wrong with this picture? The video gave vivid illustrations of the effects of depression. Then came the pitch—Brand X, sponsored by guess who? The pharmaceutical company that had produced the video. The only thing missing were free samples from a smooth sales rep. *Did anyone notice a small conflict of interest?* I wondered.

At the end of the movie, I was more horrified than angry, and in a nano-second I was in trouble. I suggested the film was no more than a push for certain drugs. The possibility that not everyone needed drugs to get through depression or crisis was nowhere to be found.

I asked, "Whatever happened to Jungian therapy and integrated treatment?" I was told my "two cents" wasn't appreciated, and my behavior wouldn't be tolerated, period! I was promptly removed from Group B.

Alone Again, Naturally

The staff systematically began to seek me out. They attempted to convince me that I was mentally ill, bipolar, and would need to be medicated for life. One after another, they assured me that my denial was typical, and I would have to agree to see it their way before I would be discharged. It was either their way or no way.

A few days later, I was allowed back into Group B. During one of the sessions, I was asked to share my story. After group, the counselor who had led the discussion spoke with me privately. He was moved by my story and wanted to know what books he could read to get more information and insight about spiritual experiences like mine. I rattled off a number of books and strongly encouraged him to venture beyond his current perspective. Finally, someone on staff was listening. A glimmer of hope!

Oh Brother, Where Art Thou?

Two challenges remained: making peace with my family and agreeing to take medication for the rest of my life. Then, I would have a chance of being discharged, but that looked so far away. Dealing with my family was the harder challenge. During one of his visits, Brad reminded me that if my insurance ran out or when it would no longer pay for a private hospital, I would be transferred to a state mental hospital. If he meant to scare me into family visits, he succeeded.

Lithium Returns

Medical residents routinely made rounds with Dr. Horowitz. They periodically attended my brief (less than fifteen minutes) therapy sessions. Dr. Horowitz or the resident would ask how I was feeling, how the meds were doing, and evaluate my progress. One of the residents—let's call him Al—was more than annoying; he was a know-it-all with the same bedside manner as Dr. Horowitz.

One day, while we were sitting in the lounge, Al came to observe us. The subject of treating alcoholism and drug addiction came up. Al mentioned that he prescribed a certain drug for alcohol and drug withdrawal, which just happened to be one of the drugs I'd sold when I worked in pharmaceuticals. Although I hadn't worked for that manufacturer for five years, I had a nearly encyclopedic recall about the drug and its FDA-approved uses. Surprising even myself, not only did I recall the indications but recited the contra-indications and precautions. The data spewed out like a computer. I reminded Al that he was using the drug "off label" (not as indicated). It was FDA-approved for hypertension, not for treating alcoholism or drug addiction.

He immediately challenged me. I just could not resist the opportunity to ruffle his feathers. Al insisted I was wrong. Things became quite heated. He refused to be corrected, and my confidence inflamed him. Adding fuel to the fire, I bet him one hundred dollars that he was wrong. The room went deadly quiet. Refusing to bet, he insisted he was right. Enough was enough. I flung a choice epithet at him, and he left. I had won the battle but was about to lose the war.

Although I had impressed my peers with my command of medical jargon and debating skills, I was in deep doo-doo. Minutes later, I was called to Dr. Horowitz's office. Al had gone directly there and told Horowitz about our argument, the bet, and my outburst.

Dr. Horowitz began by asking, "How do you think you're doing?" I answered honestly, "Quite well," and waited for his response.

He showed a rare tinge of emotion. "Honestly, I don't think you're fit for society." I was speechless. I expected a reprimand but not this. He continued, "You are still manic! Your body language, energy, and speech patterns indicate you are not in a normal state."

Seething on the inside, I did my best to remain calm and make my case. I tried to get Dr. Horowitz to see otherwise. Wasn't it obvious I had more energy than the average thirty-seven-year- old? I was in great physical shape, used to competing in long-distance swimming events and amateur triathlons. And my mother had enough energy at sixty to run circles around me. It was in my genes.

Horowitz held his ground. I was manic and that was that. He was adding Lithium to my daily medication of Depakote. Without another word, I left the room, but my heart plummeted. Lithium! The drug I hated most.

A number of the patients followed to console me. I broke down and cried. I felt violated. Who the hell were they to decide what goes in my body against my will? I'd spent months ridding myself of this toxic drug. I was trapped in the system, and my body was not my property. That evening, I was given my first dose of Lithium.

Family Counseling

I knew I'd forgive my family in time, but I wasn't ready yet. I also knew the only way out was to show Dr. Horowitz that my family could care for me after I was discharged, so I relented and told the staff I would allow family visits.

As you can imagine, even thinking about family visits brought up feelings of hurt, betrayal, and mistrust. All I could think was that I was stuck in a mental hospital because of them. Just because I allowed them to visit didn't mean I'd be "Ms. Nice" about it.

At the first visit, I let my father have it. He fell apart and even cried. After that, my brothers Brad and Larry worried that the "old man" was going to have a breakdown and asked me to go easy on him.

During a subsequent visit, my father admitted that he had made a mistake and wanted me out. He was slow to understand what I already knew—he couldn't get me out. I was the property of St. Francis Hospital. Only with a physician's consent could I be released.

Suddenly, the light came on. My father realized how screwed up the system was and told me he was getting an attorney. I was amused seeing him so panicked and uncomfortable. To his credit, he seemed determined to figure a way to get me released. In the meantime, I decided to let guilt work on him; it was a good thing.

Craig and Lynette never appeared. I suspected they knew better. But Craig did send a representative, a minister from the church I had attended. Father Marmer unexpectedly came to visit one afternoon. I was pleasantly surprised and thought he would want to talk about my spiritual transformation, especially since he had given a sermon on this topic. I asked if he knew what had happened to me. Unfortunately, I got the rote answer, "Yes, you've had a breakdown." If I could have thrown him out, I would have. The visit was over.

Visits with Brad were more uplifting. At least he wasn't caught up in diagnosing and labeling. He knew something special had happened to me, even if he wasn't able to decipher what it was. It was validating to connect with my brother this way.

Brad kept me posted on the family's counseling sessions with Horrible Horowitz. They were all beginning to see what a jerk Horowitz was. Predictably, the discussion was about keeping me on medication after discharge. Now where could that have come from? To me, this was good news. Serious discussions of my release had begun.

Please Release Me; Let Me Go

I spent a great deal of time praying for the miracle: to be released. I resented having to subdue my enthusiasm about my spiritual experience, lie about agreeing to take my medication after I was discharged, and lie about the fact that I would continue to communicate with family members. The false assumptions and injustice of it enraged me.

On Tuesday of the fourth week, I called Unity Church, an organization that published *The Daily Word*, a book of inspirational daily meditations I read regularly. Unity had a twenty-four-hour prayer line and had been a source of consolation for me in the past. As I made my prayer request, I felt a strong bond with the woman on the phone. I knew something was going to change.

Early Dismissal

By Thursday I was completing Week Four at the hospital. At about three o'clock in the afternoon, Dr. Horowitz unexpectedly called me to his office. I recall his words vividly. "I don't know why I am discharging you, but I am," he said. "Your family will be notified, and you can arrange to leave tomorrow." He went on about my behavior and the medications I would have to agree to, but I wasn't listening to the details. Blah, blah, blah. I sat in disbelief. I couldn't imagine what had transpired over the past two days to warrant this. Was it a twist of fate, or had my prayers been answered?

Word of Dr. Horowitz's decision quickly spread. Everyone wanted to know the scoop. With St. Francis's stringent discharge policy, his motivation was a mystery. There was a systematic approach to granting a discharge. Patients talked about receiving certain privileges, which usually meant being a step closer to release. For example, participation in recreational or extracurricular activities was a good sign that you were on your way. The next level was being allowed to go outside the hospital, and so forth. Patients always knew where they stood in relation to getting out. According to that logic, I figured I'd be stuck in St. Francis's for many more weeks. I had no recreational or ground privileges. I hadn't seen the outside world for four weeks. What did I do to deserve this? I was clueless.

D-Day

Friday, February 9, 1997, the day of my discharge, was emotionally charged. Janet had quite a difficult time. She cried and told me how much I had helped her. I was overwhelmed by her genuineness. She insisted on giving me her doll Bernie, the favorite of her alter Tommy. I was so touched, but I knew how much this meant to him and returned it, emphasizing my sincere appreciation. Something told me she would need Bernie a lot more than I would.

Saying goodbye to the other patients, I was gripped with sadness and empathy for them. I felt a flood of emotions: fear, apprehension, separation anxiety. Ironically, I was leaving a place where I was needed and supported by the patients, a place that had somehow felt safe in a lot of ways, and a place where my peers treated me with respect. Now I would have to face a different reality. As I packed, I considered the repercussions of returning to my life. I couldn't imagine how difficult coming home was going to be.

My father came to pick me up. I was still furious with him, but I knew this was not the time to vent my feelings. It was still too soon; my emotions were too raw. I would need time to heal from the injustice and trauma of four weeks in confinement. I pushed my feelings aside. It was time to go.

Dr. Horowitz requested I speak with him privately. Clearly, he didn't want anyone else to hear what he had to say. I followed him into his office and sat down.

He shared a story about meeting a good friend, a pianist, a few nights earlier. Speaking to her made him think about me. She had mentioned a book by Kurt Vonnegut that paralleled my situation, and this had made him think. Then he delivered the bomb. "Given the time that I have observed you, Lauren, and the remarkable change in your attitude and behavior, I've concluded that perhaps you did have a spiritual experience." At first I thought he was placating me. I just sat there in disbelief. When he offered to treat me as an outpatient and take me off Lithium, I knew he was serious. Then he discharged me.

I walked confidently as I left his office but was bewildered within. Here was the chief of the hospital telling me in his professional opinion I would not need to be medicated, even though he felt he had to say it in private. I knew he would never enter this in my records. I couldn't prove he said it. Only he and I would know the real truth. I didn't know whether to smile or insult him for cowardice.

As I was saying some final goodbyes, the alarm went off, and I saw Janet being restrained and taken to the Quiet Room.

Chapter 10:
AFTERMATH

Although four weeks seemed like a long time, in retrospect, time flew. Every day was an adventure, another scene for "my movie." I had found a new part of me—gathering friends for morning prayers, hanging out in order to help people during the day, and closing the day with evening get-togethers.

I also hoped that my presence at St. Francis woke up the staff. Since Dr. Horowitz had acknowledged my experience, perhaps he would begin to question his dogmatic approach to mental illness openly and consider integrating spirituality into patient care. If even some part of this was accomplished as a result of my stay in the hospital, then it was worth it.

Going Home

A great deal of healing was needed. I had to integrate all that had happened since the blizzard and return to my life, my home, and a demanding job. I had to work through my desire to get even, retaliate, and blame family and others. How would I manage to forgive everyone?

From the beginning of my kundalini awakening, I had heard the clear voice of my higher self. It had consistently reminded me that the higher purpose of this experience was to provide me with opportunities to choose love and forgiveness. While I would feel hurt, pain, and anger long afterwards, this was not what I was to take away from the hospitalization. I would vividly remember it forever as part of one of the most significant growth opportunities of my life. Because of that, I would eventually be able to, and even want to, forgive everyone.

When I returned home, however, I did not feel like it. I had one week to find a therapist or Dr. Horowitz would take over my outpatient care. I couldn't let that happen!

I immediately set up an appointment to see my former therapist Sandy. Not only had I sensed his presence during my hospital stay, I had spoken to him on the phone. In that conversation, I received the validation I needed. It's hard to explain, but after being released, I needed to hear that I wasn't crazy, that I really had experienced a spiritual breakthrough. I needed someone who believed in me and understood. That person was Sandy. But Sandy was not a psychiatrist and wouldn't qualify as my outpatient therapist, so the search continued.

John Dad, the Role Model for Psychiatrists

Sandy recommended Christina and Stanislav Grof's book, *Spiritual Emergency: When Personal Transformation Becomes a Crisis*. At the end of the book was a phone number for the Spiritual Emergency Network. I called and got the name of a psychiatrist in my area. From the moment we spoke on the phone, I knew John Dad (his nickname) could help me. I successfully submitted his name as my psychiatrist of record for outpatient care. Hooray! I had severed my ties with the hospital and Dr. Horowitz.

John Dad was a gentleman in every sense of the word, soft-spoken and loving, with a great, generous heart (he loved to hug). He was seventy years young. In contrast to sessions with Dr. Wachs and Horowitz, our sessions were conversational, relaxed, and open. I could discuss anything with him, and he openly shared his own thoughts and feelings. He was authentic.

He was also unusual in that he questioned most mainstream treatments. He thought holistic therapy, including nutrition and exercise, must be part of psychiatric treatment. He felt it was important to eliminate environmental toxins—you couldn't even wear perfume to his office. And he was livid about the circumstances of my hospitalization and the treatment I received.

He didn't treat me like a patient but as a respected colleague. He laughed and cried with me. He expressed and mirrored my feelings. He wasn't afraid to explore his emotions with me. He was a thinking, feeling human being, atypical from mainstream psychiatrists. That's what made him so amazing. He acted as my guide and coach, exactly what I had prayed for. I knew that with John Dad I could safely integrate the transformation that had begun with my kundalini experience.

Post-traumatic Stress

I felt compelled to forgive my family and friends, but I was filled with anxiety. John Dad explained that these feelings were symptoms of post-traumatic stress disorder caused by the shock of hospitalization. Being forced into the hospital, he said, was a catastrophic event. Add to that the stress of getting back into the routine of life, and that diagnosis was not a stretch. John Dad felt it was imperative to deal first with my hospital experience, returning to work, and my personal life. There would be time for forgiveness later.

It is worth noting that John Dad did not like to label patients. He asked if I was comfortable with his diagnosis of post-traumatic stress disorder, the mildest condition he could submit to the insurance companies. It was a huge relief and a great start for our relationship.

Off the Meds

John Dad, of course, supported my decision not to be medicated and was furious that I had been placed on them against my will. He weaned me off the medication slowly, and by the time I returned to work, I was drug-free and back to using holistic modalities with John Dad to integrate and process all that had happened.

Back to Work

I went back to work after just two weeks, but I had no idea that returning would be harder to deal with than either the kundalini awakening or the hospitalization. Word had gotten around, and a number of my clients knew I had been hospitalized. Rumors had spread quickly. How would I act in a world where people thought I had a breakdown, even though I knew I had had a breakthrough? I have a confession to make: My confidence was shaken.

I also knew I no longer belonged in this type of job. The all-consuming nature of it no longer worked for me. I needed a plan to get out. With John Dad's blessing, I decided to go to school to prepare for a new career. In the hopes of opening up a holistic wellness center, I enrolled in cosmetology and aesthetician (skin care) school in May, three months after my discharge. Classes would be twenty hours a week for one year, and I'd have to continue working full-time. Who would have thought that at thirty-seven, with a college degree, I'd be in beauty school? Hey—a vision is a vision!

Reconciliation Begins

In May, as I started school, a crisis with my brother Michael once again forced regular contact with my family. Michael had hit rock bottom with his drinking, and he called for help; he knew he was self-destructing. John Dad and I decided it was a good time to begin working toward forgiveness with my whole family.

The first step was to feel the anger, and then take the sting out of it using one of several techniques. John Dad assured me that by processing my anger and my hurt feelings in sessions with him, I would eventually be able to move past it. Every session began with deep breathing and relaxation. As sessions developed, John Dad might intuitively suggest a rebirthing session, a guided meditation, or even hypnosis, all with the goal of helping me discover the essence of my anger.

Although John Dad was all about love, he offered no emotional shortcuts. Sessions with him were far from gentle. Letting my emotions out—anger, hurt, and sense of betrayal—required lots of yelling, cursing, and screaming. Let's say I took the F-word to a whole new level. And the best part was when John Dad joined in. He was right there with me. "Yeah," he might say, "fuck 'em. Get angry! Get pissed off." I yelled (or cried) until I had exhausted that emotion—until the anger didn't matter anymore—at least for that session. I never knew there were so many shades of anger.

Next, we began to differentiate old, repressed anger from the recent anger caused by my hospitalization. This was an effective tool for diffusing the rage I was feeling. John Dad explained that oftentimes a kind of snowball effect can occur with family members or people with whom we have a history. In other words, differentiating the anger around my hospitalization from my childhood- or adolescent-repressed anger would diffuse the intensity of the emotions I was feeling.

The second step was developing compassion for the people who hurt me most. John Dad used role reversal or psychodrama techniques to help me. I took on the role of each of my family members and explored their emotions. I would empathize with them and reenact what I imagined they had experienced.

He also explored each family member's history and background through me. What was it like for my father, as a boy, to find his parents dead? Then, as an adult, to have his sister, then his daughter placed in an institution. How would it feel to be a mother whose only daughter was having a breakdown? These exercises helped further diffuse the outrage and anger I felt. I could see how our past affects our future, how and why my parents did what they did. I could see how we are doomed to repeat our mistakes if we do not heal them.

Finally, I was able to explore the consequences of my own actions and take responsibility for them. It became clearer that while my "outburst" at St. Francis may have felt great at the time, my "act" also had grave consequences. In other words, don't act nuts in a nuthouse!

Through John Dad, I learned how important it was to have a guide on my journey toward healing. The seeds of forgiveness had started to germinate within me.

Moving On

Forgiveness, to John Dad, was a selfish act, the right kind of selfishness. He taught me to feel compassion for the very people I was emotionally not ready to forgive. Now I could see the possibility of forgiving those I blamed. John Dad said that the purpose of forgiveness was to let me move on; the added benefit was to the other people involved. It wasn't about making my family right; it wasn't about making me forget. Forgiving would allow me to heal and move through the anger. I could leave behind the tragedy of the experience and celebrate the beautiful transformation that had been interrupted.

My work with John Dad helped me decide not to pursue any legal action against St. Francis. I concluded it would have been too emotionally costly. In the end, writing a book and a screenplay would prove more cathartic—and a lot more fun!

Applying Forgiveness

Michael went into a dual-diagnosis rehab facility for a little more than a month, and I had to deal with my family. The family had to step in for his outpatient care. My brothers handled the financial end, but it would be up to my mother and me to tend to his emotional needs. Of course, Conchetta, the great caretaker, cooked his meals, cleaned his apartment, and shopped for him. I took him to appointments and got him out of his apartment. I remembered my friend George had asked me to "take care of Michael," during his visit in January.

While helping Michael, I spent a great deal of time with my mother. Despite loving her very much, I was still angry with her. But I knew it was time to develop a healthier relationship. I would no longer consent to participate in the same dynamics we had in the past. There was a new me, and I was determined to express it.

My awakening had profoundly shifted my dependency on my mother. I felt free to express my opinions and beliefs whether she agreed or not, and I no longer felt guilty for having them. Our boundaries were clear, which was an enormous breakthrough for me. The umbilical cord had finally been cut. As I became more accepting of her, I was also getting closer to the vision I'd always had of me—the confident woman in black.

At the beginning of 1998, I celebrated the first anniversary of my hospitalization by staying the course. I remained focused on graduating and kept the vision of my book and movie before me. The driving force was to get out of the competitive, stressful workplace, cut myself lose from the beeper, and create a business that incorporated aesthetics, spirituality, beauty, and healing in a place where I could help women empower themselves from the inside out.

In May, I graduated from cosmetology school and was able to leave the corporate world.

The New Seminary

At the suggestion of friends, I enrolled in an interfaith seminary in September 1998, and for two years, I continued on my spiritual journey and deepened my spiritual practice. The course material was challenging, and the process of inner growth was powerful. It forced me to look at myself in a new way, to walk my talk, to serve others, and to live the best life I could.

John Dad, Farewell

In February 2000, shortly before ordination, I received a letter from John Dad. It was addressed to all his patients, telling us he was closing his practice due to illness and moving to Texas with his daughter. In March, I received a second letter expressing his appreciation and love for all of us. He said this would be the last time I would be hearing from him.

In April, I received a letter from his daughter saying that he had passed away. I attended a memorial service near his home in Newtown, Connecticut, in May. I had not fully grasped the impact of his presence in my life. He was the perfect person to guide my transition to a fuller life. He had a beautiful spirit and was a tremendous gift to me. It took some time to process and grieve this loss.

John Dad's death removed the safety net. I was back in charge of my own spiritual, mental, and emotional well-being, and I continued to use his holistic approach. The lesson? Everything happens for a reason and for the best.

It Was All Worth It

Where am I all these years later? I believe I've come a long way. Through ongoing energy work, spiritual practice, and emotional and psychological healing that began with John Dad, I have learned a valuable and essential lesson: I am responsible for my life. I know that I will never again be chronically depressed.

Oh, I still experience the ups and downs of life. I occasionally have periods of expanded awareness, and the same foot vibrates as it did in 1996; I have become more psychic, intuitive, and clear.

Like most everyone else, I also have days of feeling depressed, where I feel that my life is not where I want it, but depression is no longer a way of life. Instead, it's a message that I'm not in balance, that I'm too stressed, or that I'm focusing too much in one area of my life. I use it as a gauge, an internal barometer to help assess what I need. I embrace it and think kindly of it, for it is now my teacher.

The bottom line is: my spiritual awakening changed me at a cellular level forever. My essence has been altered. On the outside, I probably appear much the same (perhaps younger- looking, thanks to my present job in the aesthetic industry!). Yet, I have been transformed. I know it. And that is another key. I am the only one who has to be convinced; there is no one else I need to prove anything to. During times when I feel challenged, I can return to the experience of the winter of 1996. Misdiagnosis and hospitalization, thank God, were not able to take any of it away. It didn't take away my family either.

Family Restored

I'm pleased to say that today my family life has returned to normal, whatever that means. My brothers and I are still Type A personalities, self-confident, independent business people, and we enjoy getting together with our families. My parents have remained divorced and do not see each other unless required to be at the same gathering, but I have good relationships with both of them.

Unfortunately, Michael passed away in July of 2005, after suffering two years from multiple strokes, which eventually took his life. I truly believe the combination of years of alcohol abuse, cigarettes, medications, and poor diet were to blame. At the end of his life, Michael constantly reminded me to write "our book", so here it is, Michael!

Seven years ago, I met Andy, my lover, lifetime partner, and best friend. For the first time, my family has accepted and embraced my significant other, and that is a true blessing.

Finally

When I promised John Dad I would share my story with others who have gone through similar experiences, I never thought it would take so many years. I have finished what I set out to do. I am concerned about the controversial message: the medical paradigm has to change. Not everyone needs to be medicated, and more importantly, medication is not the first step toward healing. Before admission to a mental hospital, people must be evaluated to differentiate spiritual awakenings from pathological disturbances. The psycho-spiritual connection must be acknowledged and incorporated into Western methods of diagnosis and treatment. That is my mission and the purpose for writing this book.

I often think of Jack Kornfield's book, *After the Ecstasy, Now the Laundry*. There's been a lot of laundry since my kundalini rising, for sure. I leave with words written by Harry R. Moody, Ph.D., and David Carroll in *The Five Stages of the Soul*:

> "Experiencing a spiritual breakthrough leaves its mark on a person forever…. Yet, as the Zen proverb tells us: 'Before enlightenment, we chop wood and carry water. After enlightenment, we chop wood and carry water.'"

And life goes on.

Epilogue:
A LETTER TO MY FRIENDS IN THE HOSPITAL

To My Hospital Friends:

I have thought of you often during these past years. I wonder how you are, where you might be, and if you are well. I pray you are flourishing.

The truth is, all of us can use help at almost any time in our lives, the same way we can all use prayer, contemplation, and meditation—like we did together in the hospital. Do you remember the positive changes so many of us made just by adding in the spiritual component, by sharing, journaling, and talking deep into the night? Many of us needed that spiritual connection and community more than any medication. I think we still need it.

I understand now why so many psychiatric patients are "repeaters." I wrote Chapter 10 to address that challenge and to give you or someone you know hope. It was difficult to put the hospitalization behind me. Even with my transformational experience, I still needed help from John Dad and others. It took two years to process and integrate this life-changing event. I still believe that almost everyone I met in the hospital could be released if spiritual counseling were available to them.

My dear friends, when others fear New Age hocus pocus or quackery, ask them to look at the research and writings of transpersonal psychiatrists and practitioners. There are other treatments; no one should be misdiagnosed any longer. Our medical system can do better.

I salute you on the rest of your journey. May your travels be light and joyful. Peace to you.

Love,
Lauren

Appendix
DSM-IV RELIGIOUS & SPIRITUAL PROBLEMS

David Lukoff, Ph.D.

The work of Dr. David Lukoff, Stanislav and Christina Grof and others in the field of transpersonal psychology[13] and psychiatry has successfully defined and distinguished spiritual emergencies. Dr. Lukoff's groundbreaking research, online courses

---

[13] Transpersonal psychology is a type of psychology or psychotherapy that focuses on altered states of consciousness and transcendent experiences as a means to understanding the human mind and treating mental disorders. Transpersonal psychology emphasizes meditation, prayer, and self-transcendence. Etymology: coined by Carl Jung (1917) *Webster's New Millennium™ Dictionary of English, Preview Edition (v 0.9.6) Copyright © 2003-2005 Lexico Publishing Group, LLC.*

and writings established him as a leading authority in the field of transpersonal psychology and spiritual emergence. His research provides the best resource material I have found to date (go to www.spiritualcompetency.com). Most of this section will highlight Dr. Lukoff's actual research on spiritual emergence and emergency/crisis.

Dr. Lukoff has written, taught, and worked as a transpersonal psychiatrist for many years, and authored a substantial amount of material on the subject of diagnosing spiritual emergencies. His writing on the subject is so thorough, with his permission, we have reprinted his article, "From Spiritual Emergency to Spiritual Problem: The Transpersonal Roots of the New DSM-IV Category," *Journal of Humanistic Psychology*, 38(2), 21–50, 1998 (www.spiritualcompetency.com).

The inclusion in the *DSM-IV* of a new diagnostic category called "Religious or Spiritual Problem" marks a significant break-through. For the first time, there is acknowledgment of distressing religious and spiritual experiences as non-pathological problems. Spiritual emergencies are crises during which the process of growth and change becomes chaotic and overwhelming. The proposal for this new diagnostic category came from transpersonal clinicians concerned with the misdiagnosis and mistreatment of persons in the midst of spiritual crises.

Abstract of Dr. Lukoff's Research

Religious or Spiritual Problem is a new diagnostic category (Code V62.89) in the *Diagnostic and Statistical Manual—Fourth Edition* (APA, 1994). While the acceptance of this new category was based on a proposal documenting the extensive literature on the frequent occurrence of religious and spiritual issues in clinical practice, the impetus for the proposal came from transpersonal clinicians whose initial focus was on spiritual emergencies—forms of distress associated with spiritual practices and experiences. The proposal grew out of the work of the Spiritual Emergence Network to increase the competence of mental health professionals in sensitivity to such spiritual issues. This article describes the rationale for this new category, the history of the proposal, transpersonal perspectives on spiritual emergency, types of religious and spiritual problems (with case illustrations), differential diagnostic issues, psychotherapeutic approaches, and the likely increase in number of persons seeking therapy for spiritual problems. It also presents the preliminary findings from a database of religious and spiritual problems.

Introduction

"Religious or Spiritual Problem" is a new diagnostic category (Code V62.89) in the *Diagnostic and Statistical Manual–Fourth Edition* (APA, 1994). The Thesaurus of Psychological Index Terms (Walker, 1991) states that religiosity "is associated with religious organizations and religious personnel" (p. 184) whereas spirituality refers to the "degree of involvement or state of awareness or devotion to a higher being or life philosophy. Not always related to conventional religious beliefs" (p. 208). Thus religious problems involve a person's conflicts over the beliefs, practices, rituals and experiences related to a religious institution. Some forms of spirituality presume no external divine or transcendent forces (e.g., humanistic-phenomenological spirituality) (Elkins, Hedstrom, Hughes, Leaf, and Saunders, 1988), and spiritual problems involve distress associated with a person's relationship to a higher power or transcendent force that is not related to a religious organization.

While the acceptance of this new category was based on a proposal documenting the extensive literature on the frequent occurrence of religious and spiritual issues in clinical practice, the impetus for the proposal came from transpersonal clinicians whose initial focus was on spiritual emergencies—forms of distress associated with spiritual practices and experiences. The proposal grew out of the work of the Spiritual Emergence Network (Prevatt and Park, 1989) to increase the competence of mental health professionals in sensitivity to such spiritual issues. This article describes the rationale for this new category, the history of the proposal that was presented to the Task Force on DSM-IV, transpersonal perspectives on spiritual emergency, types of spiritual problems (with case illustrations), differential diagnostic issues, therapeutic approaches for spiritual problems, and the likely increase in number of persons seeking therapy for spiritual problems.

Rationale for a New Diagnostic Category

Prevalence of Religious and Spiritual Problems

In a survey of APA member psychologists, 60% reported that clients often expressed their personal experiences in religious language, and that at least 1 in 6 of their patients presented issues which directly involve religion or spirituality (Shafranske & Maloney, 1990). Another study of psychologists found 72% indicating that they had at some time addressed religious or spiritual issues in treatment (Lannert, 1991). In a sample that included psychologists, psychiatrists, social workers, and marriage and family therapists, 29% agreed that religious issues are important in the treatment of all or many of their clients (Bergin & Jensen, 1990). Anderson and Young (1988) claim that: "All clinicians inevitably face the challenge of treating patients with religious troubles and preoccupations" (p. 532). While little is known about the prevalence of specific types of religious and spiritual problems in treatment, these surveys demonstrate that religious and spiritual issues are often addressed in psychotherapy.

Lack of Training in Religious and Spiritual Issues

In a survey of Association of Psychology Internship Centers training directors, 83% reported that discussions of religious and spiritual issues in training occurred rarely or never. One hundred percent indicated they had received no education or training in religious or spiritual issues during their formal internship. Most of the training directors did not read professional literature addressing religious and spiritual issues in treatment, and they stated that little was being done at their internship sites to address these issues in clinical training (Lannert, 1991). A national study of APA member psychologists found that 85% reported rarely or never having discussed religion and spiritual issues during their own training (Shafranske & Maloney, 1990). Similar findings from other surveys suggest that this lack of training is the norm throughout the mental health professions (Sansone, Khatain & Rodenhauser, 1990).

Ethical Mandate to Provide Training

According to the Ethical Principles of Psychologists and Code of Conduct (American Psychological Association, 1992), psychologists have an ethical responsibility to be aware of social and cultural factors which may affect assessment and treatment (Canter, Bennet, Jones & Nagy, 1994). Since the religious and spiritual dimensions of culture are among the most important factors that structure human experience, beliefs, values, behavior as well as illness patterns (James, 1958; Krippner & Welch, 1992), sensitivity to religious and spiritual issues is an important part of the cultural diversity competence of psychologists. Certain issues in differential diagnosis require knowledge of the patient's religious subgroup (Lovinger, 1984) and/or the nature of acceptable expressions of subculturally validated forms of religious expression. For example, discussing one of the cases in the DSM-III-R Casebook, Spitzer, Gibbon & Skodol (1989) noted that, "The central question in the differential diagnosis in this case is whether or not the visions, voices, unusual beliefs, and bizarre behavior are symptoms of a true psychotic disorder ... [or] Can this woman's unusual perceptual experiences and strange notions be entirely accounted for by her religious beliefs?" (pp. 245-6). Similarly, distinguishing between a spiritual problem and psychopathology requires knowledge about spiritual beliefs, practices and their effects (Lukoff, 1985).

In the training of psychiatrists, such preparation is now required by the Accreditation Council for Graduate

Medical Education. Their "Special Requirements for Residency Training in Psychiatry" published in 1995 mandates instruction about gender, ethnicity, sexual orientation, and religious/spiritual beliefs in accredited residency training programs. Psychologists are also required to be aware of their need for training (Canter et al., 1994). Unfortunately, the current APA accreditation guidelines for graduate training programs and internships do not directly address competency in addressing religious and spiritual diversity, despite indications that the training of psychologists is inadequate in this area (Lannert, 1991).

Psychologists are also required to provide services only within their boundaries of competence (Canter et al., 1994). The surveys reviewed above show that psychologists are very likely to work with the religious and spiritual issues of their clients. Yet their lack of training in the assessment and treatment of religious and spiritual problems may lead to insensitivity and/or countertransference issues that interfere with their ability to understand and explore their clients' issues (Meyer, 1988; Shafranske & Gorsuch, 1984; Strommen, 1984). In addition, there are unique ethical issues involved in working with spiritual problems, especially those that involve altered states of consciousness (Taylor, 1995). Ignorance, counter-transference, and lack of skill can impede the untrained psychologist's ethical provision of therapeutic services to clients who present with spiritual problems.

History of the Proposal for Religious or Spiritual Problem

The initial impetus for this proposal came from the Spiritual Emergence Network (then called the Spiritual

Emergency Network), which was concerned with the mental health system's pathologizing approach to intense spiritual crises. The authors decided to propose a new diagnostic category for the then-in-development DSM-IV as the most effective way to increase the sensitivity of mental health professionals to spiritual issues in therapy. A previous article in the *Journal of Transpersonal Psychology* (Lukoff, 1985) had proposed a new diagnostic category entitled Mystical Experience with Psychotic Features (MEPF) for intense spiritual experiences that present as psychotic-like episodes. An analogy was drawn between MEPF and the DSM-III-R category of Uncomplicated Bereavement, which is a V Code—a condition *not attributable to a mental disorder*. The definition for this category notes that even when the period of bereavement following a significant loss meets the diagnostic criteria for Major Depression, this diagnosis is not given because the symptoms result from "a normal reaction to the death of a loved one" (p. 361). Similarly, individuals in the midst of a tumultuous spiritual experience (a "spiritual emergency") may appear to have a mental disorder if viewed out of context, but are actually undergoing a "normal reaction" which warrants a nonpathological diagnosis (i.e., a V Code for a condition not attributable to a mental disorder) (Lukoff, 1988a).

Following this precedent of bereavement in DSM-III-R of a nonpathological category for a distressing and disruptive experience, we notified the American Psychiatric Association's Task Force on DSM-IV in early 1991 of our intention to submit a proposal for a new V Code category entitled "Psychospiritual Conflict." We contacted other experts in the field, including several members of APA's Division 36 (Psychology of Religion), to obtain their support and suggestions for relevant research and case studies. We also conducted several literature searches on PsychINFO, Medline and Religion Index to obtain references to clinical and research literature (Lukoff, Turner & Lu, 1992; Lukoff, Turner & Lu, 1993). At the 1991 and 1992 Association for Transpersonal Psychology Conferences, we presented our ideas for the new category and received useful suggestions from other transpersonally-oriented psychologists and psychiatrists.

As the proposal evolved, we substituted "problem" for "conflict" to be more in line with the terminology employed in the V Code section of DSM-III-R (e.g., Parent-Child Problem, Phase of Life Problem). To obtain greater support for the proposal and to acknowledge the many areas of overlap between spirituality and religion, we expanded our proposal to include both psychospiritual and psychoreligious problems. The literature review established the most prevalent and clinically significant problems within each category, enabling us to arrive at the following definition for a proposed V Code:

> *Psychoreligious problems* are experiences that a person finds troubling or distressing and that involve the beliefs and practices of an organized church or religious institution. Examples include loss or questioning of a firmly held faith, change in denominational membership, conversion to a new faith, and intensification of adherence to religious practices and orthodoxy. *Psychospiritual problems* are

experiences that a person finds troubling or distressing and that involve that person's relationship with a transcendent being or force. These problems are not necessarily related to the beliefs and practices of an organized church or religious institution. Examples include near-death experience and mystical experience. This category can be used when the focus of treatment or diagnosis is a psychoreligious or psychospiritual problem that is not attributable to a mental disorder.

In December 1991, the proposal for Psychoreligious or Psycho-spiritual Problem was formally submitted to the Task Force on DSM-IV. The proposal stressed the need for this new diagnosis to improve the cultural sensitivity of the DSM-IV since this was one of the priorities established for the revision (Frances, First, Widiger, Miele, Tilly, David, & Pincus, 1991), and also argued that the adoption of this new category would result in the following benefits: 1) increasing the accuracy of diagnostic assessments when religious and spiritual issues are involved; 2) reducing the occurrence of iatrogenic harm from misdiagnosis of religious and spiritual problems; 3) improving treatment of such problems by stimulating clinical research; and 4) improving treatment of such problems by encouraging training centers to address religious and spiritual issues in their programs. Support for the proposal was obtained from the American Psychiatric Association Committee on Religion and Psychiatry and the NIMH Workgroup on Culture and Diagnosis. The proposal in its entirety was published in the *Journal of Nervous and Mental Disease* (Lukoff, Lu & Turner, 1992). In January 1993, the Task Force accepted the proposal but changed the title to "Religious or Spiritual Problem" and shortened and modified the definition to read:

> This category can be used when the focus of clinical attention is a religious or spiritual problem. Examples include distressing experiences that involve loss or questioning of faith, problems associated with conversion to a new faith, or questioning of other spiritual values which may not necessarily be related to an organized church or religious institution. (American Psychiatric Association, 1994, p. 685)

Articles on this new category appeared in *The New York Times* (Steinfels, 1994), *San Francisco Chronicle* (Lattin, 1994), *Psychiatric News* (McIntyre, 1994), and the *APA Monitor* (Sleek, 1994), where it was described as indicating an important shift in the mental health profession's stance toward religion and spirituality. What did not receive attention in the media is that this new diagnostic category has its roots in the transpersonal movement's attention to spiritual emergencies.

Transpersonal Perspectives on Spiritual Emergency

Assagioli (1989), in his seminal paper, "Self-Realization and Psychological Disturbances," noted the association between spiritual practices and psychological problems.

For example, persons may become inflated and grandiose as a result of intense spiritual experiences: "Instances of such confusion are not uncommon among people who become dazzled by contact with truths too great or energies too powerful for their mental capacities to grasp and their personality to assimilate" (p. 36). Stanislav and Christina Grof coined the term "spiritual emergency" and founded the Spiritual Emergency Network (Prevatt & Park, 1989) in 1980 to identify a variety of psychological difficulties, particularly those associated with Asian spiritual practices that entered the West starting in the 1960's. They define spiritual emergencies as:

> ...crises when the process of growth and change becomes chaotic and overwhelming. Individuals experiencing such episodes may feel that their sense of identity is breaking down, that their old values no longer hold true, and that the very ground beneath their personal realities is radically shifting. In many cases, new realms of mystical and spiritual experience enter their lives suddenly and dramatically, resulting in fear and confusion. They may feel tremendous anxiety, have difficulty coping with their daily lives, jobs, and relationships, and may even fear for their own sanity (Grof & Grof, 1989, back cover)

Grof and Grof (1989) note that "Episodes of this kind have been described in sacred literature of all ages as a result of meditative practices and as signposts of the mystical path" (p. x). They have described the more common presentations including: mystical experiences, kundalini awakening (a complex physio-psychospiritual transformative process observed in the Yogic tradition) (Greenwell, 1990), shamanistic initiatory crisis (a rite of passage for shamans-to-be in indigenous cultures, commonly involving physical illness and/or psychological crisis) (Lukoff, 1991; Silverman, 1967), possession states (Lukoff, 1993) and psychic opening (the sudden occurrence of paranormal experiences) (Armstrong, 1989). Their list of types has expanded from an initial typology of 8 to currently some 12 types, although in actual clinical practice there is often overlap between these types. A distinguishing characteristic of spiritual emergencies is that despite the distress, they can have very beneficial transformative effects on individuals who experience them. Several types of spiritual emergency are illustrated below. The diagnostic formulation of Psychospiritual Conflict in the initial development of the proposal for a new category was specifically intended to be inclusive of persons undergoing spiritual emergencies.

Case Study Database on Religious and Spiritual Problems

While there is limited psychological theory that is useful in understanding spiritual problems, there is an extensive knowledge base that has developed at the case level. Kazdin (1982) has observed, "Although each case is studied individually, the information is accumulated to identify more general relationships" (p. 8). Bromley (1986) likens this to the building up of case-law in jurisprudence, which

> ...provides rules, generalizations and categories which gradually systematize the knowledge (facts and theories) gained from the intensive study of individual cases. Case-law (theory, in effect) emerges through a process of conceptual refinement as successive cases are considered in relation to each other. (p.2)

Despite the disrepute in which case studies are generally held (i.e., case study methods are rarely taught in the research methods courses in graduate psychology programs), they are still a primary mode of transmitting knowledge (Hunter, 1986). Grand rounds and intake presentations are two institutionalized forms by which health professionals disseminate the latest understandings and make links between the generalized abstractions of diagnostic categories and a particular patient. In addition, case studies play a significant role in advancing knowledge by focusing on anomalies that highlight inadequacies in understanding, diagnosis and treatment (Churchill & Churchill, 1982). Case study findings have played a pivotal role in the evolution of academic psychology and particularly psychotherapy (Edwards, 1991; Kazdin, 1982). In transpersonal psychology (Boorstein, 1980; Chinen, 1988; Lukoff, 1988b) and humanistic psychology (Bugental, 1990; Schneider & May, 1995; Yalom, 1989) as well, published case studies have guided the development of assessment and therapeutic approaches.

Cases where a focus of therapy involves a religious or spiritual problem are not very easy to find. A systematic analysis of case reports involving religious or spiritual issues the Medline bibliographic database from 1980–1996 located only 364 abstracts that addressed religious or spiritual issues in health care. This was from a database containing 4,306,906 records from this period (Glazer, National Library of Medicine, personal communication, May 1997), indicating that a shockingly low .008% of published articles in the major medical health care database address religious and spiritual issues. Through multiple searches on PsycINFO and Medline, over 100 cases that describe religious and spiritual problems have been located (Lukoff et al., 1992; Lukoff et al., 1993). No claim is made that the numbers of cases in the database shown in table 1 are representative of the prevalence of cases seen in clinical practice. They are probably more indicative of the types of problems that mental health professionals like to write about. In addition, the quality of the case reports varies widely. Few use any checks for reliability or validity (Yin, 1993). But as Bugental (1995) has noted:

> Writing about the work of psychotherapy is challenging, apt to slide into oversimplification, difficult to keep to a consistent level of specificity or abstraction, and vulnerable to manipulation. Nevertheless, it is important to bring the experiences of our consultation rooms into our literature and to attempt to convey the uncommunicable, the subtle interplay between two human beings trying to work with and improve the life experience of one (or both?) of them. (p. 102)

Table 1. Numbers of Cases in Database by Type

Religious Problems

Number	Type
4	Change in denomination/Conversion
5	Intensification of religious belief or practice
12	Loss of faith
5	Joining or leaving a New Religious Movement or cult
5	Other religious problem

Spiritual Problems

2	Loss of faith
4	Near-death experience
2	Mystical experience
3	Kundalini
4	Shamanistic Initiatory Crisis
2	Psychic opening
2	Past lives
2	Possession
4	Meditation-related
2	Separating from a spiritual teacher
2	Other spiritual problem

Combined Religious/Spiritual Problem

17	Serious illness
6	Terminal illness

Overlap of Religious/Spiritual Problem and DSM-IV Disorder

2	Religious/spiritual problem concurrent with substance abuse
7	Religious/spiritual problem concurrent with psychotic disorder
2	Religious/spiritual problem concurrent with mood disorder
1	Religious/spiritual problem concurrent with dissociative disorder
1	Religious/spiritual problem concurrent with obsessive-compulsive disorder

Types of Religious Problems

The most common examples of religious problems described in the clinical literature include loss or questioning of faith, change in denominational membership or conversion to a new religion, intensification of adherence to the beliefs and practices of one's own faith, and joining, participating or leaving a new religious movement or cult. Usually people undergo such changes without any significant psychological difficulty, but the clinical literature documents cases of individuals who experience significant distress and seek mental health assessment and treatment for these problems. Discussions and clinical examples of religious problems can be found in Lukoff et al. (1992), Lukoff, Lu & Turner (1995), and Turner, Lukoff, Barnhouse & Lu (1985). This article focuses on types of spiritual problems, including spiritual emergencies, that have been identified, particularly in the literature in transpersonal psychology. Below summaries of published case studies are used to illustrate the key differential diagnostic and treatment issues involved in several types of spiritual problems.

Types of Spiritual Problems

Questioning of Spiritual Values: The DSM-IV definition notes that spiritual problems may be related to questioning of spiritual values. In the clinical literature, many cases that involve a questioning of spiritual values are triggered by an experience of loss of a sense of spiritual connection. Barra, Carlson and Maize (1993) conducted a survey study and also reviewed the anthropological, historical, and contemporary perspectives on loss as a grief-engendering phenomenon. They found that loss of religious or spiritual connectedness,

> ...whether in relation to traditional religious affiliation or to a more personal search for spiritual identity, frequently resulted in individuals experiencing many of the feelings associated with more "normal" loss situations. Thus, feelings of anger and resentment, emptiness and despair, sadness and isolation, and even relief could be seen in individuals struggling with the loss of previously comforting religious [or spiritual] tenets and community identification. (p. 292)

Loss of faith is mentioned in the DSM-IV definition as a religious problem, but as Barra et al. (1993) note, the same sequalae can result from the loss of spiritual connection. One case which involved questioning of spiritual values was described by Emma Bragdon (1994).

> In 1971, Emma's mother, then 56, was living alone in a small town Vermont, and working as a visiting nurse. She was a Zen Buddhist practicing meditation 6–8 hours daily. Her friends noticed that she was spending more time alone and was becoming increasingly emotionally labile. They contacted Emma, but she did not sense a problem since she was having cheerful talks on the telephone with her mother about plans for her mother to visit during the birth of Emma's first child. However, before this happened, Emma's mother went into the woods alone, reading a passage from *Zen Mind, Beginner's Mind* where Suzuki Roshi compares enlightenment to physical death. When found dead, her finger was pointing to this passage. She had cut her wrists and throat.
>
> In addition to the bereavement over her mother's suicide, this loss also triggered a spiritual problem for Emma, who was herself a practicing Zen Buddhist. How could her spiritual path lead to her mother's suicide? Emma contacted Suzuki Roshi, who flew with her to Vermont where he conducted a traditional Buddhist funeral ceremony. During this time, Emma had a number of powerful spiritual experi-

ences, including feeling herself engulfed in white light accompanied by ecstatic release. She sensed that her mother was fine, and that her passing had been a happy occasion for her. But afterwards, when back in California, she began to have doubts. How did she really know her mother was okay? As she became preoccupied with questioning the validity of her spiritual experiences and tenets, she also wondered if she was crazy. When it was 10 days past her due date, she went into her garden to pray, and made a commitment to stop questioning her spiritual beliefs until 2 months after giving birth. One hour later, she reports she went into labor. (adapted from pp. 171-177)

During this period, Emma was in turmoil as she questioned her spiritual beliefs and path. The guidance of a spiritual teacher, Suzuki Roshi, and spiritual practices, such as praying, played an important role in helping her to resolve these conflicts.

Meditation-related Problems

Asian traditions recognize a number of pitfalls associated with intensive meditation practice, such as altered perceptions that can be frightening, and "false enlightenment," associated with delightful or terrifying visions (Epstein, 1990). Epstein (1990) describes a "specific mental disorder that the Tibetans call 'sokrlung' (a disorder of the 'life-bearing wind that supports the mind' that can arise as a consequence... of strain[ing] too tightly in an obsessive way to achieve moment-to-moment awareness" (p. 27). When meditative practices are transplanted into Western contexts, the same problems can occur. Anxiety, dissociation, depersonalization, altered perceptions, agitation, and muscular tension have been observed in western meditation practitioners (Bogart, 1991; Walsh & Roche, 1979). Yet Walsh and Roche (1979) point out that "such changes are not necessarily pathologic and may reflect in part a heightened sensitivity" (p. 1086). The <u>DSM-IV</u> emphasizes the need to distinguish between psychopathology and meditation-related experiences: "Voluntarily induced experiences of depersonalization or derealization form part of meditative and trance practices that are prevalent in many religions and cultures and should not be confused with Depersonalization Disorder" (p. 488).

Kornfield (1993), a psychologist and experienced meditation teacher, described what he termed a spiritual emergency that took place at an intensive meditation retreat he was leading.

> An "overzealous young karate student" decided to meditate and not move for a full day and night. When he got up, he was filled with explosive energy. He strode into the middle of the dining hall filled with 100 silent retreatants and began to yell and practice his karate maneuvers at triple speed. Then he screamed, "When I look at each of you, I see behind you a whole trail of bodies showing your past lives." As an experienced meditation teacher,

Kornfield recognized that the symptoms were related to the meditation practice rather than signs of a manic episode (for which they also meet all the diagnostic criteria except duration). The meditation community handled the situation by stopping his meditation practice and starting him jogging, ten miles in the morning and afternoon. His diet was changed to include red meat, which is thought to have a grounding effect. They got him to take frequent hot baths and showers, and to dig in the garden. One person was with him all the time. After three days, he was able to sleep again and was allowed to started meditating again, slowly and carefully. (adapted from pp. 131–132)

Mystical Experience

The definitions of mystical experience used by researchers and clinicians vary considerably, ranging from Neumann's (1964) "upheaval of the total personality" to Greeley's (1974) "spiritual force that seems to lift you out of yourself" to Scharfstein's (1973) "everyday mysticism." A definition of mystical experience both congruent with the major theoretical literature and clinically applicable is as follows: the mystical experience is a transient, extraordinary experience marked by feelings of unity, harmonious relationship to the divine and everything in existence, as well as euphoria, sense of noesis (access to the hidden spiritual dimension), loss of ego functioning, alterations in time and space perception, and the sense of lacking control over the event (Allman, De La Roche, Elkins & Weathers, 1992; Hood, 1974; Lukoff & Lu, 1988).

Numerous surveys assessing the incidence of mystical experience (Allman et al., 1992; Back & Bourque, 1970; Gallup, 1987; Hood, 1974; Spilka, Hood & Gorsuch, 1985; Thomas & Cooper, 1980) indicate that 30–40% of the population have had mystical experiences, suggesting that they are normal rather than pathological phenomena. While mystical experiences are associated with lower scores on psychopathology scales and higher psychological well-being than controls (Greeley, 1974), case studies document instances where mystical experiences are disruptive and distressing. This is one type of spiritual problem that psychologists see regularly. In a survey, psychologists reported that 4.5% of their clients over the past 12 months brought a mystical experience into therapy (Allman et al., 1992). In the first case below, the mystical experience led to a spiritual problem, but not a spiritual emergency.

> A woman in her early thirties sought out therapy to deal with unresolved parental struggles and guilt over a younger brother's psychosis. Approximately two years into her therapy, she underwent a typical mystical experience, including a state of ecstasy, a sense of union with the universe, a heightened awareness transcending space and time, and a greater sense of meaning and purpose to her life. For ten days, she remained in an ecstatic state. She felt that everything in her life had led up

to this momentous experience and that all her knowledge had become reorganized during its course. Due to the rapid alteration in her mood and her unusual ideation, her therapist considered diagnoses of mania, schizophrenia, and hysteria. But he rejected these because many aspects of her functioning were either unchanged or improved, and overall her experience seemed to be "more integrating than disintegrating... While a psychiatric diagnosis cannot be dismissed, her experience was certainly akin to those described by great religious mystics who have found a new life through them" (p. 806).

This experience increasingly became the focus of her continued treatment, as she worked to integrate the insights and attitudinal changes that followed. The therapist reported that the most important gain from it was a conviction that she was a worthwhile person with worthwhile ideas, not the intrinsically evil person, 'rotten to the core, 'that her mother had convinced her she was. Her subsequent treatment focused on expanding the insights she had gained and on helping her to integrate the mystical experience (adapted from *Group for the Advancement of Psychiatry*, 1976).

The second case (Lukoff & Everest, 1985) fits the spiritual emergency model in that the mystical experience led to a crisis, which resulted in hospitalization and medication that probably were not necessary.

> At age 19, after returning home from hitchhiking in Mexico, Howard became convinced that he was on a "Mental Odyssey." To his family and friends, he began speaking in a highly metaphorical language. For example, after returning from a simple afternoon hike up a mountain, he announced to his parents that "I have been through the bowels of Hell, climbed up and out, and wandered full circles in the wilderness. I have ascended through the Portals of Heaven where I established my rebirth in the earth itself, and now have taken my rightful place in the Kingdom of Heaven." To one friend, he stated: "I am the albatross; you are the dove." The unusual actions and content of his speech led his family to commit him to a psychiatric ward where he was diagnosed with acute schizophrenia.
> Once admitted to the hospital, Howard asked to see a Jungian therapist, but this request was ignored and he was given thorazine. While in the hospital, he continued his self-proclaimed odyssey by drawing elaborate "keys" that were mandalas stocked with many well-known symbols and cultural motifs, including the Islamic crescent and star, the yin yang symbol, the infinity sign, and pierced hands, eyes, and

circles. In the hospital, he also conducted elaborate self-designed "power" rituals and rituals to the four directions, despite being on high doses of medication. After two months in the psychiatric hospital, his psychiatrist wanted to transfer him to a long-term facility for further treatment, but he refused to go and was discharged. He left feeling totally exhausted, physically and emotionally, but he continued exploring the mythological, philosophical and artistic parallels to his "Mental Odyssey." He read works by Joseph Campbell and C. G. Jung and joined a "New Age" religious group where he encountered many similar motifs.

In the subsequent 24 years, he has not been hospitalized or on medication, has held positions as an operator of high-tech video editing equipment, and completed a college degree. When interviewed 11 years after the episode for a case study, he maintained that "I have gained much from this experience. I am sorry for the worry and hurt that it may have caused my family and friends. These wounds have been slow to heal. I am deeply grateful for the great victory of my odyssey. From a state of existential nausea, my soul now knows itself as part of the cosmos. Each year brings an ever increasing sense of contentment." (adapted from Lukoff and Everest, 1985, pp. 127–143)

The mystical nature of his experience is evidenced by his euphoria, intense sense of noesis, and feeling of direct connection to transcendent forces. He also had the several of the prognostic signs indicating that a positive outcome would be likely: acute onset, good pre-episode functioning, and exploratory attitude (Lukoff, 1985). Thus he serves as an example of how a spiritual emergency client, who in all likelihood could have been treated on outpatient basis without medication, was unnecessarily and inappropriately hospitalized.

Near-Death Experience (NDE)

The NDE is a subjective event experienced by persons who come close to death, who are believed dead and unexpectedly recover, or who confront a potentially fatal situation and escape uninjured. It usually includes dissociation from the physical body, strong positive affect, and transcendental experiences. Phenomenologically, there is a characteristic temporal sequence of stages: peace and contentment; detachment from physical body; entering a transitional region of darkness; seeing a brilliant light; and passing through the light into another realm of existence) (Greyson, 1983). While only 1/3 of persons who survive an encounter with death have this type of NDE (Ring, 1990), modern medical technology has resulted in many persons experiencing NDEs. In 1982, Gallup estimated that approximately eight million American adults have had a NDE with at least some of the features described above.

Although positive personality transformations frequently follow a NDE, significant intrapsychic and interpersonal difficulties may also arise (Greyson & Harris,

1987). Many individuals report that they doubted their mental stability, and therefore did not discuss the NDE with friends or professionals for fear of being rejected, ridiculed, or regarded as psychotic or hysterical. One person reported, "I've lived with this thing [NDE] for three years and I haven't told anyone because I don't want them to put the straitjacket on me" (Sabom & Kreutziger, 1978, p. 2). A hospitalized patient recounted that "I tried to tell my nurses what had happened when I woke up, but they told me not to talk about it, that I was just imagining things" (Moody, 1975, p. 87). Even religious professionals have not always been sensitive to the spiritual dimensions of such experiences: "I tried to tell my minister, but he told me I had been hallucinating, so I shut up" (Moody, 1975, p. 86).

Fortunately, the many published scientific articles and first person accounts have resulted in greater sensitivity to these experiences (Basford, 1990; Kason & Degler, 1994). NDEs are recognized as fairly common occurrences in modern ICUs, as is the need to differentiate between ICU psychoses and NDEs, and the importance of not "treating" NDEs with antipsychotic medication (Greyson & Harris, 1987). In a recent publication, Greyson (1997) described the distress associated with NDEs as a Religious or Spiritual Problem and noted that, "The inclusion of this new diagnostic category in the DSM-IV permits differentiation of NDEs and similar experiences from mental disorders and may lead to research into more effective treatment strategies" (p. 327).

Leaving a Spiritual Teacher or Path

Persons transitioning from the "culture of embeddedness" with their teachers into more independent functioning often seek psychotherapeutic help (Bogart, 1992). Vaughan (1987) reports that many individuals who have left destructive spiritual teachers reported that the experience ultimately contributed to their wisdom and maturity through meeting the challenge of restoring their integrity. One such case was described by Bogart (1992):

> Robert had spent 8 years as the disciple of a teacher from an Asian tradition that emphasized surrender and obedience. Robert had become one of the teacher's attendants, and reported that he "Loved the teacher very much." Yet there were difficulties. The guru frequently embarrassed Robert publicly, humiliating him in front of large classes and castigating him for incompetence. He even physically beat Robert in private. But Robert didn't rebel and hoped that by continuing to remain under the teacher's guidance, he might yet win great praise, confirmation, or sponsorship from his mentor that would enable him to advance spiritually.
> Robert left the community after the guru's sexual and financial misconduct were revealed. Upon leaving, he had intense and at times even paralyzing feelings of betrayal, anger, fear, worthlessness and guilt. Robert went into psychotherapy with a spiritually sensitive therapist. Later in psychotherapy, he realized that his relationship with the guru replicated his relationship with his father—an angry

alcoholic who had humiliated and physically injured Robert, but whose approval he had nevertheless sought. He also worked on major issues around establishing a life outside the structure of the spiritual community and integrating his spiritual beliefs and practices into this new life (adapted from pp. 4–5, 16–17).

Spiritual Emergence

In spiritual *emergence,* (another term from the transpersonal psychology literature), there is a gradual unfoldment of spiritual potential with minimal disruption in psychological/social/occupational functioning, whereas in spiritual *emergency* there is significant abrupt disruption in psychological/social/occupational functioning. The Benedictine monk, Brother David Steindl-Rast, describes the process: "Spiritual emergence is a kind of birth pang in which you yourself go through to a fuller life, a deeper life, in which some areas in your life that were not yet encompassed by this fullness of life are now integrated or called to be integrated or challenged to be integrated" (cited in Bragdon, 1994, p. 18). While less disruptive than spiritual emergencies, emergence can also lead persons to seek out a therapist to help integrate their new spiritual experiences (Grof, 1993).

Differential Diagnosis Between Mental Disorders and Spiritual Emergencies

Making the differential diagnosis between a spiritual emergency and psychopathology can be difficult because the unusual experiences, behaviors and visual, auditory, olfactory or kinesthetic perceptions characteristic of spiritual emergencies can appear as the symptoms of mental disorders: delusions, loosening of associations, markedly illogical thinking, or grossly disorganized behavior. For example, the jumbled speech of someone trying to articulate the noetic quality of a mystical experience can appear as loose associations. Or the visions of a NDE can appear as hallucinations. Or the need for solitude and quiet of a person in a spiritual emergency can appear as catatonia or depression-related withdrawal (Bragdon, 1993). Wilber (1993) argues that the distinction between spiritual emergencies and psychopathology hinges on the critical distinction between pre-rational states and authentic trans-personal states. The "pre/trans fallacy" involves confusing these conditions, which is easy to do. "Since both prepersonal and transpersonal are, in their own ways, nonpersonal, then prepersonal and transpersonal tend to appear similar, even identical, to the untutored eye" (Wilber, 1993, p. 125).

Lending further credibility to the existence of spiritual emergency as a valid clinical phenomenon, there is considerable overlap among the criteria proposed by different authors for making the differential diagnosis between psychopathology and spiritual emergencies. These constants include: 1) cognitions and speech thematically related to spiritual traditions or to mythology; 2) openness to exploring the experience; 3) no conceptual disorganization (Buckley, 1981; Grof & Grof, 1989; Lukoff, 1985; Watson, 1994). Lukoff (1985a) suggested using good prognostic signs to help distinguish between psychopathology and spiritual emergencies, including: 1) good pre-episode functioning; 2) acute onset of symptoms during a period of three months or less; 3) stressful precipitants to the psychotic episode; and 4) a positive exploratory attitude toward the experience. These criteria have been validated in numerous outcome studies from psychotic episodes (reviewed in Lukoff [1985a]), and would probably also identify individuals who are in the midst of a spiritual emergency with psychotic features that has a high likelihood of a positive outcome.

Spiritual Problems Concomitant With DSM-IV Mental Disorders

All of the cases of spiritual problems described above are not mental disorders, nor associated with coexisting mental disorders. But clients may also present with spiritual problems that are associated with mental disorders. The DSM-IV, specifically notes that an individual can be diagnosed with both a mental disorder and a related problem, as long as "the problem is sufficiently severe to warrant independent clinical attention" (p. 675). Thus, for example, Religious or Spiritual Problem could be coded *along with* Bipolar Disorder (both on Axis I) if the religious/spiritual content (frequently observed in manic states [Goodwin & Jamison, 1990; Podvoll, 1990]) is also addressed during treatment of a manic episode. This greatly expands the potential usage of this category since the symptoms and treatment of many mental disorders include religious and spiritual content, especially substance abuse disorders (where the treatment frequently includes 12-step programs) and psychotic disorders, although dissociative, mood, and obsessive compulsive disorders often present with significant religious and spiritual issues as well (Robinson, 1986).

Psychotherapeutic Approaches for Spiritual Problems

First it should be noted that religious and spiritual experiences usually are not distressing to the individual and do not require treatment of any kind. However, some spiritual conflicts do lead persons to seek therapy. There are published cases studies illustrating sensitive ways to conduct psychotherapy utilizing a wide range of therapeutic approaches (e.g., psychoanalytic [Finn & Gartner, 1992], cognitive-behavioral [Propst, 1980], transpersonal [Chinen, 1988]). Rational emotive therapy is one exception where published material consistently shows a hostile attitude toward spirituality and religion (e.g., Ellis, 1980).

However, for spiritual emergencies, most of the models of intervention come from the transpersonal psychology literature. Grof and Grof (1990) recommend that the person temporarily discontinue active inner exploration and all forms of spiritual practice, change their diet to include more "grounding foods" (such as red meat), become involved in very simple grounding activities (such as gardening), engage in regular light exercise (such as walking), and use expressive arts (such as drawing, clay and evocative music) to allow the expression of emotions and experiences through color, forms, sound and movement. In the case described above, Kornfield made use of most of these elements to avoid hospitalizing the individual who entered a spiritual emergency during a meditation retreat. Reliance on the client's self-healing capacities is one of the main principles that guides transpersonal treatment of spiritual emergencies (Perry, 1974; Watson, 1994). In addition, psychologists should be willing to consult, work closely with or even refer to spiritual teachers who may have considerably more expertise in the specific types of crises associated with a given spiritual practice or tradition. Unfortunately mental health professionals rarely consult with religious professionals or spiritual teachers even when dealing religious and spiritual issues (Larson, Hohmann, Kessler, Meador, Boyd, & McSherry, 1988).

Another key component of treatment of spiritual emergencies is normalization of and education about the experience. While this is a common technique in therapy, it plays an especially important role with spiritual emergencies because persons in the midst of spiritual emergencies are often afraid that the unusual nature of their expcriences indicates that they are "going crazy" (as described in some of the above cases). An extremely abbreviated version of normalization of an unusual spiritual experience is reported by Jung (1964) in the following case:

> I vividly recall the case of a professor who had a sudden vision and thought he was insane. He came to see me in a state of complete panic. I simply took a 400-year-old book from the shelf and showed him an old woodcut depicting his very vision. "There's no reason for you to believe that you're insane," I said to him. "They knew about your vision 400 years ago." Whereupon he sat down entirely deflated, but once more normal. (p. 69)

A complete mind/body/spirit integrated approach to spiritual emergencies would also make use of alternative therapeutic treatments such as diet, bodywork, exercise and movement, homeopathy, herbs (just to name a few) (Bragdon, 1993: Cortright, 1997). There may even be times when medication can play a role in recovery and integration of these experiences.

Increasing Incidence of Spiritual Experiences and Problems

On virtually all measures, there has been a major decline in the strength of the mainstream religious institutions and confidence in religion and religious leadership in American culture (Princeton Religious Research Center, 1985; Stark & Bainbridge, 1985). While 70% of Americans report in Gallup polls that they attend church regularly (Gallup, 1987), a recent study of the actual religious behavior of Americans found that half of persons who tell pollsters that they attend church regularly are not telling the truth. Kosmin and Lachman (1993) conducted an in depth interview study (rather than a simple poll as has been used in most studies) with 4,001 randomly selected individuals about the nature and frequency of church attendance, and membership in a denomination. By also tracking attendance at churches, they found that only 19% of adult Americans regularly practice their religion. Some 22.5% exhibit "only trace elements" of religion in their lives; another 29% were rated as barely or nominally religious, and 7.5% describe themselves as agnostics. The researchers concluded that most Americans claim a religion that does not significantly inform their attitudes or behavior.

Yet at the same time people are turning away from conventional religious institutional forms, the number of people who report that they personally believe in God or some spiritual force, who pray or engage in some spiritual practice, and who report a mystical experience has been increasing. In one survey, 75% of persons who are not members of a church or synagogue say that they pray sometime during their everyday lives, and 58% of Americans reported the need to experience spiritual growth (Woodward, 1994). During the last 25 years, there has been a significant increase in people adopting spiritual practices, including a wide array of meditation, martial arts, tai chi, chanting, and yoga techniques. There has also been an explosion of interest in mystical, esoteric, shamanic and pagan traditions that involve participation in sweat lodges, goddess circles and the rituals of many small new spiritual schools and "New Age Groups" (Lewis & Melton, 1992). Twelve step programs, with their focus on a "higher power" and spiritual awakening, have been developed for a wide-range of problems and have millions of adherents. Psychospiritually-oriented cancer support groups are another recent phenomenon.

Gallup polls (1987) have shown an increase in percentages of people who report: mystical experiences (from 35% in 1973 to 43% in 1986), contact with the dead (from 27% in 1973 to 42% in 1986), ESP (from 58% in 1973 to 67% in 1986), visions (from 8% in 1973 to 29% in 1986) and other unusual experiences. Based on his 15 years of survey research, Greeley (1987) concluded, "More people than ever say they've had such experiences ... whether you look at the most common forms of psychic and mystical experience or the rarest

... [t]hese experiences are common, benign and often helpful. What has been 'paranormal' is not only becoming normal in our time—it may also be health-giving" (p.49). Even such unusual experiences as UFO abductions (Ring, 1992), paranormal (Braud, 1995; Hastings, 1983), and out-of-the-body experiences (Gabbard & Twemlow, 1984) are often experienced as meaningful, positively transformative, and spiritual. Accordingly, as the number of persons who engage in spiritual practices and have spiritual experiences increases, it seems likely that the incidence of spiritual problems seen in psychotherapy will also grow.

Conclusion

To date, religious problems have received much more attention than spiritual problems in the clinical and research literature. There is a handbook (Wicks, Parsons & Capps, 1993) and about a dozen journals devoted to pastoral counseling, several more to "Christian psychiatry," as well as professional organizations and conferences that address religious problems. There are no journals focused on spiritual problems. Transpersonal psychologists actively investigate both spiritual experiences that are trans, beyond our ordinary personal and biological self, and also spiritual practices such as Zen Buddhism and Patanjali Yoga, which are designed to lead to intense spiritual experiences (Rao, 1995). While transpersonal psychology is avowedly nonsectarian (Lajoie & Shapiro, 1992), many transpersonal psychologists are hopeful that the systematic study of these spiritual practices and their associated experiences can facilitate their occurrence in their clients (when clinically appropriate) (Tart, 1995). But this requires sensitivity to the types of problems that are also associated with specific practices.

Religious and spiritual problems need to be subjected to more research to better understand their prevalence, clinical presentation, differential diagnosis, outcome, treatment, relationship to the life cycle, ethnic factors and predisposing intrapsychic factors. While defining discrete religious and spiritual problems for study clearly presents difficulties, such as the frequent overlap in the categories discussed above, the extensive and rigorous research on the phenomenology, prevalence, outcome, clinical sequalae, treatment of NDEs serves as a model demonstrating that the obstacles are not insurmountable (Greyson, 1983, 1997; Greyson & Harris, 1987; Ring, 1990, 1992). The acceptance of religious and spiritual problems as a new diagnostic category in DSM-IV is a reflection of increasing sensitivity to cultural diversity in the mental health professions and of transpersonal psychology's impact on mainstream clinical practice.

References

Agosin, T. (1992). Psychosis, dreams and mysticism in the clinical domain. In F. Halligan & J. Shea (Eds.), *The fires of desire*, New York: Crossroad.

Allman, L. S., De La Roche, O., Elkins, D. N., & Weathers, R. S. (1992). Psychotherapists's attitudes towards clients reporting mystical experiences. *Psychotherapy*, 29, 564-569.

American Psychiatric Association. (1994). *Diagnostic and statistical manual, fourth edition*. Washington, D.C.: American Psychiatric Association.

American Psychological Association. (1992). *Ethical Principles of Psychologists and Code of Conduct*. Washington, DC: American Psychological Association.

Anderson, R. G., & Young, J. L. (1988). The religious component of acute hospital treatment. *Hospital and Community Psychiatry*, 39, 528-555.

Armstrong, A. (1989). The challenge of psychic opening: A personal story. In S. Grof & C. Grof (Eds.), *Spiritual emergency: When personal transformation becomes a crisis*, Los Angeles: J. P. Tarcher.

Assagioli, R. (1989). Self-realization and psychological disturbances. In S. Grof & C. Grof (Eds.), *Spiritual emergency: When personal transformation becomes a crisis*. Los Angeles: Tarcher.

Back, K., & Bourque, L. (1970). Can feelings be enumerated? *Behavioral Science*, 15, 487-496.

Barra, D., Carlson, E., & Maize, M. (1993). The dark night of the spirit: Grief following a loss in religious identity. In K. Doka & J. Morgan (Eds.), *Death and spirituality*. Amityville, NY: Baywood.

Basford, T. K. (1990). *Near-death experience*. New York: Garland.

Bergin, A., & Jensen, J. (1990). Religiosity of psychotherapists: A national survey. *Psychotherapy*, 27, 3-7.

Bogart, G. (1991). The use of meditation in psychotherapy. *American Journal of Psychotherapy*, 45(3), 383-412.

Bogart, G. C. (1992). Separating from a spiritual teacher. *Journal of Transpersonal Psychology*, 24(1), 1-22.

Boorstein, S. (Ed.). (1980). *Transpersonal psychotherapy*. Palo Alto, CA: JTP Books.

Bragdon, E. (1993). *A sourcebook for helping people with spiritual problems*. Aptos, CA: Lightening Up Press.

Braud, W. (1995). Parapsychology and spirituality: Implications and intimations. *ReVision: A Journal of Consciousness and Transformation*, 18(1), 36-43.

Bromley, D. (1986). *The case-study method in psychology and related disciplines.* New York: John Wiley & Sons.

Buckley, P. (1981). Mystical experience and schizophrenia. *Schizophrenia Bulletin*, 7, 516-521.

Bugental, J. (1990). *Intimate journeys: Stories from life-changing therapy.* San Francisco: Jossey-Bass.

Bugental, J. F. T. (1995). Context and meaning in writing case reports. *Journal of Humanistic Psychology*, 35(2), 99-102.

Canter, M. B., Bennet, B. E., Jones, S. E., & Nagy, T. E. (1994). *Ethics for psychologists: A commentary on the APA Ethics Code.* Washington, D.C.: American Psychological Association.

Chinen, A. (1988). Clinical symposium: Challenging cases in transpersonal psychotherapy. *Journal of Transpersonal Psychology*, 20(1), 1-48.

Churchill, L., & Churchill, S. (1982). Storytelling in medical arenas. *Literature and Medicine*, 1, 73-79.

Cortright, B. (1997). *Psychotherapy and Spirit: Theory and Practice in Transpersonal Psychotherapy.* Albany, NY: State University of New York Press.

Edwards, D. (1991). Duquesne phenomenological research method as a special class of case study research. In R. van Vuuren (Ed.), *Dialogue beyond polemics*, (pp. 53-70). Pretoria: Human Sciences Research Council.

Elkins, D., Hedstrom, J., Hughes, L., Leaf, A. and Saunders, C. (1988). Toward a humanistic-phenomenological spirituality. *Journal of Humanistic Psychology*, 28, 5-19.

Ellis, A. (1980). Psychotherapy and atheistic values: A response to A, E. Bergin's "Psychotherapy and Religious

Issues". *Journal of Consulting and Clinical Psychology,* 48, 635-639.

Epstein, M. (1990). Psychodynamics of Meditation: Pitfalls on the Spiritual Path. *Journal of Transpersonal Psychology,* 22(1), 17-34.

Finn, M., & Gartner, J. (Eds.). (1992). *Object relations theory and religion.* Westport, CT: Praeger.

Frances, A., First, M., Widiger, T., Miele, G., Tilly, S., David, W., & Pincus, H. (1991). An A to Z guide to DSM-IV conundrums. *Journal of Abnormal Psychology,* 100, 407-412.

Gabbard, G., & Twemlow, S. (1984). *With the eyes of the mind: An empirical analysis of out-of-the-body states.* New York: Praeger.

Gallup, G. (1982). *Adventures in immortality: A look beyond the threshold of death.* New York: McGraw-Hill.

Gallup, G. (1987). *The Gallup poll: Public opinion 1986.* Wilmington, DE: Scholarly Resources.

Goodwin, F., & Jamison, K. (1990). *Manic-depressive illness.* New York: Oxford University.

Greeley, A. (1987, January/February). Mysticism goes mainstream. *American Health,* 47-49.

Greeley, G. (1974). *Ecstacy: A way of knowing.* Englewood Cliffs, N.J.: Prentice Hall.

Greenwell, B. (1990). *Energies of transformation: A guide to the kundalini process.* Saratoga, CA: Shakti River Press.

Greyson, B. (1983). The Near-death Experience Scale: Construction, reliability and validity. *Journal of Nervous and Mental Disease,* 171, 369-375.

Greyson, B. (1997). The near-death experience as a focus of clinical attention. *Journal of Nervous and Mental Disease,* 185(5), 327-334,

Greyson, B., & Harris, B. (1987). Clinical approaches to the near-death experience. *Journal of Near-Death Studies,* 6(1), 41-52.

Grof, C. (1993). *The thirst for wholeness: Addiction, attachment, and the spiritual path.* New York: HarperCollins.

Grof, S., & Grof, C. (Eds.). (1989). *Spiritual emergency: When personal transformation becomes a crisis.* Los Angeles: Tarcher.

Group for the Advancement of Psychiatry (1976). *Mysticism: Spiritual quest or mental disorder?* New York: author.

Hastings, A. (1983). A counseling approach to parapsycholgical experience. *Journal of Transpersonal Psychology,* 15(2), 143-167.

Hood, R. W. (1974). Psychological strength and the report of intense religious experience. *Journal for the Scientific Study of Religion,* 13, 65-71.

Hunter, K. (1986). "There was this one guy...": The use of anecdotes in medicine. *Perspectives in Biology and Medicine,* 29, 619-630.

James, W. (1958). *The varieties of religious experience.* New York: New American Library of World Literature.

Jung, C. G. (1964). Approaching the unconscious. In C.G. Jung (Ed.), *Man and his symbols.* London: Aldus Books.

Kason, Y., & Degler, T. (1994). *A farther shore: How near-death and other extraordinary experiences can change ordinary lives.* Toronto: HarperCollins.

Kazdin, A. (1982). *Single-case research designs.* New York: Oxford University Press.

Kornfield, J. (1993). *A path with heart: A guide through the perils and promises of spiritual life.* New York: Bantam Books.

Kosmin, B., & Lachman, S. (1993). *One nation under God: Religion in contemporary America.* New York: Harmony.

Krippner, S., & Welch, P. (1992). *Spiritual dimensions of healing.* New York: Irvington Publishers.

Lajoie, D., & Shapiro, S. (1992). Definitions of transpersonal psychology: The first 23 years. *Journal of Transpersonal Psychology,* 24(1), 79-98.

Lannert, J. (1991). Resistance and countertransference issues with spiritual and religious clients. *Journal of Humanistic Psychology,* 31(4), 68-76.

Larson, D., Hohmann, A., Kessler, L., Meador, K., Boyd, J., & McSherry, E. (1988). The couch and the cloth: The need for linkage. *Hospital and Community Psychiatry,* 39(10), 10641069.

Lattin, D. (1994, March 17, 1994). Therapists turn from psyche to soul. *San Francisco Chronicle,* pp. A1, 12.

Lewis, J., & Melton, T. (Eds.). (1992). *Perspectives on the New Age.* Albany, NY: State University of New York Press.

Lovinger, R. (1984). *Working with religious issues in therapy.* New York: Aronson.

Lukoff, D. (1985). The diagnosis of mystical experiences with psychotic features. *Journal of Transpersonal Psychology,* 17(2), 155-181.

Lukoff, D. (1988a). Transpersonal perspectives on manic psychosis: Creative, visionary, and mystical states. *Journal of Transpersonal Psychology,* 20(2), 111-139.

Lukoff, D. (1988b). Transpersonal therapy with a manic-depressive artist. *Journal of Transpersonal Psychology,* 20(1), 10-20.

Lukoff, D. (1991). Divine madness: Shamanistic initiatory crisis and psychosis. *Shaman's Drum,* 22, 24-29.

Lukoff, D. (1993). Case study of the emergence of a contemporary shaman. In R. I. Heinze (Ed.), *Proceedings of the Ninth International Conference on Shamanism and Alternate Healing.* Berkeley, CA: Asian Scholars Press.

Lukoff, D. (1995, August). Findings From a Database of Religious and Spiritual Problems. Paper presented at the meeting of the American Psychological Society, New York, NY.

Lukoff, D., & Everest, H. C. (1985). The myths in mental illness. *Journal of Transpersonal Psychology,* 17(2), 123-153.

Lukoff, D., & Lu, F. (1988). Transpersonal psychology research review: Mystical experience. *Journal of Transpersonal Psychology,* 21(1), 161-184.

Lukoff, D., Lu, F., & Turner, R. (1992). Toward a more culturally sensitive DSM-IV: Psychoreligious and Psychospiritual Problems. *Journal of Nervous and Mental Disease,* 180(11), 673-682.

Lukoff, D., Lu, F., & Turner, R. (1995). Cultural considerations in the assessment and treatment of religious and spiritual problems. *The Psychiatric Clinics of North America,* 18(3), 467-485.

Lukoff, D., Turner, R., & Lu, F. (1992). Transpersonal psychology research review: Psychoreligious dimensions of healing. *Journal of Transpersonal Psychology,* 24(1), 41-60.

Lukoff, D., Turner, R., & Lu, F. G. (1993). Transpersonal psychology research review: Psychospiritual dimensions of healing. *Journal of Transpersonal Psychology,* 25(1), 11-28.

McIntyre, J. (March 4, 1994). Psychiatry and Religion: A visit to Utah. *Psychiatric News,* 29, 12.

Meyer, M. S. (1988). Ethical principles of psychologists and religiosity. *Professional Psychology: Research and Practice*, 19(5), 486-488.

Moody, R. (1975). *Life after life.* New York: Bantam.

Neumann, E. (1964). Mystical man. In J. Campbell (Ed.), *The mystic vision,* Princeton, NJ: Princeton University Press.

Perry, J. (1974). *The far side of madness.* Englewood Cliffs, NJ: Prentice Hall.

Podvoll, E. (1990). *The seduction of madness: Revolutionary insights into the world of psychosis and a compassionate approach to recovery at home.* New York: HarperCollins.

Prevatt, J., & Park, R. (1989). The Spiritual Emergence Network (SEN). In S. Grof & C. Grof (Eds.), *Spiritual emergency: When personal transformation becomes a crisis,* (pp. 225-232). Los Angeles: J. P. Tarcher.

Princeton Religious Research Center. (1985). *Religion in America.* Princeton, NJ: author.

Propst, L. R. (1980). The comparative efficacy of religious and nonreligious imagery for the treatment of mild depression in religious individuals. *Cognitive Therapy and Research*, 4(2), 167-178.

Rao, K. R. (1995). Some reflections on religion and anomalies of consciousness. *ReVision: A Journal of Consciousness and Transformation*, 18(1), 11-17.

Ring, K. (1990). *Life at death: A scientific investigation of the near-death experience.* New York: Coward, McGann & Geoghegan.

Ring, K. (1992). *The Omega Project: Near-death, UFO encounters, and mind at large.* New York: William Morris.

Robinson, L. (Ed.). (1986). *Psychiatry and religion: Overlapping concerns.* Washington, DC: American Psychiatric Press.

Sabom, M. B., & Kreutziger, S. (1978). Physicians evaluate the near-death experience. *Theta,* 6, 1-6.

Sansone, R., Khatain, K., & Rodenhauser, P. (1990). The role of religion in psychiatric education: A national survey. *Academic Psychiatry,* 14, 34-38.

Scharfstein, B. (1973). *Mystical experience.* New York: Bobbs-Merrill.

Schneider, K., & May, R. (1995). *The psychology of existence.* New York: McGraw-Hill.

Shafranske, E., & Maloney, H. (1990). Clinical psychologists' religious and spiritual orientations and their practice of psychotherapy. *Psychotherapy,* 27, 72-78.

Shafranske, E. P., & Gorsuch, R. L. (1984). Factors associated with the perception of spirituality in psychotherapy. *Journal of Transpersonal Psychology,* 16, 231-241.

Silverman, J. (1967). Shamans and acute schizophrenia. *American Anthropologist,* 69(1), 21-31.

Sleek, S. (1994, June). Spiritual problems included in DSM-IV. *American Psychological Association Monitor,* 17.

Spilka, B., Hood, R., & Gorsuch, R. (1985). *The psychology of religion: An empirical approach.* Englewood, N.J.: Prentice-Hall.

Spitzer, R., Gibbon, M., & Skodol, A. (1989). *DSM-III-R Casebook.* Washington, DC: American Psychiatric press.

Stark, R., & Bainbridge, W. (1985). *The future of religion.* Berkeley, CA: University of California Press.

Steinfels, P. (1994, Feb. 10, 1994). Psychiatrists' manual shifts stance on religious and spiritual problems. *New York Times,* pp. A9.

Strommen, M. P. (1984). Psychology's blind spot: A religious faith. *Counseling and Values,* 28, 150-161.

Tart, C. (1995). World Parliament of superstition: Scientific evidence for a basic reality to the spiritual.

ReVision: A Journal of Consciousness and Transformation, 18(1), 3-10.

Taylor, K. (1995). *The ethics of caring: Honoring the web of life in our professional healing relationships.* Santa Cruz, CA: Hanford Mead Publishers.

Thomas, L., & Cooper, P. (1980). Incidence and psychological correlates of intense spiritual experiences. *Journal of Transpersonal Psychology,* 12(1), 75-85.

Turner, R., Lukoff, D., Barnhouse, R., & Lu, F. (1985). Religious and spiritual problem: A culturally sensitive diagnostic category in the DSM-IV. *Journal of Nervous and Mental Disease,* 183(7), 435-444.

Vaughan, F. (1987). A question of balance: Health and pathology in new religious movements. In D. Anthony, B. Ecker, & K. Wilber (Eds.), *Spiritual choices: The problem of recognizing authentic paths to inner transformation,* (pp. 265-282). New York: Paragon House.

Walker, A. (Ed.). (1991). *Thesaurus of Psychological Terms (2nd ed.).* Arlington, VA: American Psychological Association.

Walsh, R., & Roche, L. (1979). Precipitation of acute psychotic episodes by intensive meditation in individuals with a history of schizophrenia. *American Journal of Psychiatry,* 136, 1085-1086.

Watson, K. W. (1994). Spiritual emergence: Concepts and implications for psychotherapy. *Journal of Humanistic Psychology,* 34(2), 22-45.

Wicks, R., Parsons, R., & Capps, D. (Eds.). (1993). *Clinical handbook of pastoral counseling.* Mahwah, NJ: Paulist Press.

Wilber, K. (1993). The pre/trans fallacy. In R. Walsh & F. Vaughan (Eds.), *Paths beyond ego,* (pp. 124-130). Los Angeles: Tarcher.

Woodward, K. (1994, 28 December). The search for the sacred: America's search for spiritual meaning. *Newsweek*.

Yalom, I. D. (1989). *Love's executioner and other tales of psychotherapy*. New York: HarperCollins.

Yin, R. (1993). *Applications of Case Study Research*. Newbury Park, CA: Sage.

Made in the USA
Charleston, SC
18 December 2009